Help!

Help!: The Art of Computer Technical Support
Ralph Wilson

Peachpit Press
2414 Sixth Street
Berkeley, CA 94710
510/548-4393
510/548-5991 (fax)

The twelve guidelines for effective complaints which appear in Chapter 7 are reprinted from *The Frozen Keyboard: Living with Bad Software* by Boris Belzer (TAB Books, 1988) with permission of the author.

Library of Congress Cataloging-In-Publication Data
Wilson, Ralph
Help!: the art of computer technical support / Ralph Wilson.
p. cm.
ISBN 0-938151-14-2: $19.95
1.   Computer service industry—United States—Management.
2.   Market surveys—United States. I. Title.
HD9696.C63U5956 1991
004'.068'—dc20   90-48737
     CIP

ISBN 0-938151-14-2

0 9 8 7 6 5 4

  Printed on Recycled Paper

Printed and bound in the United States of America

Help!
The Art of Computer Technical Support

by Ralph Wilson

Illustrated by Mari Stein

An Open House Book

Peachpit Press
Berkeley, California

Help!: The Art of Computer Technical Support
© 1991 Ralph Wilson

Peachpit Press
2414 Sixth Street
Berkeley, CA 94708
510/548-4393 or 800/283-9444

The twelve guidelines for effective complaints which appear in Chapter 7 are reprinted from The Frozen Keyboard: Living with Bad Software *by Boris Beizer (TAB Books, 1988) with permission of the author.*

Library of Congress Cataloging-in-Publication Data
Wilson, Ralph.
   Help!: the art of computer technical support / Ralph Wilson.
   p. cm.
   ISBN 0-938151-14-2: $19.95
   1.   Computer service industry—United States—Management.
   2.   Market surveys—United States. I. Title.
   HD9696.C63U5956 1991
   004'.068'—dc20   90-48737
        CIP

Preface

For all their benefits, for all the exciting and unprecedented new power they bring, computers also cause their share of trouble. Bugs and glitches, user error and confusion, and the sheer complexity of the technology make a combination that often leads to calls for help.

This book is for the people who answer those calls, the people who do technical support. It offers practical advice and background information about a profession that's just beginning to get the attention it deserves.

Whether you work for a manufacturer helping customers on a product hotline, or for a corporation helping its employees on a computer help desk, this book is for you. If you manage one of these functions or take calls yourself, or both, there's material here that will be of interest.

What Is Tech Support?

I define technical support as *knowledgeable people assisting the users of computer hardware and software products*. The word "assisting" in the definition is important. If I teach you to use a product, that's training. If I sit down and carry out a project for you, that's consulting. If I help you with a problem you're having with your software or hardware, or answer a question, or listen to your feedback, that's tech support. There are times when the distinctions between these three fields get a little blurry, but by and large, tech support is *user assistance*.

The word "knowledgeable" in the definition is also important. Knowledge is suggested by the word "technical," which comes from the Greek *technikos,* referring to art, craft, or skill. If I try to help you with a product I don't know in some depth, I'm not doing technical support (and we're both probably wasting our time).

We'll look at various alternative modes of support in this book, but I still put "people" in my definition. Whether the user talks directly to a human being or to a machine, there's got to be a human intelligence behind the technology to qualify as tech support in my book.

Most of the support I'll discuss here is of the "hands off" variety—the person who needs the help is located at a distance from the helper, and their communication takes place over the phone or some other electronic medium. This separation is common to most support situations and it's part of the challenge of the work. Whether it's a traditional telephone hotline, an electronic bulletin board, or a fax connection, you have to find ways to bridge the gap that separates you from the person who needs your help.

Much of what's included here is equally relevant to any platform, but this book concentrates on technical support of microcomputer hardware and software products. One reason is simply that that's the area I'm most familiar with. Another is that mainframe and minicomputer support usually involves high-level technical communication between computer professionals on both ends of the line. That contrasts with microcomputer support, where your callers are likely to range from beginners to experts. Finally, mainframe and mini support is almost always done as part of a costly service arrangement, so the economics of the game are much different. If you do mainframe or mini support, or even do support on noncomputer products, you should find many useful ideas here, though you won't find much attention to the specific setting you work in.

Where I'm Coming From

This book is based on my experience doing and managing technical support for the last five years, as well as on interviews with many people in the field.

I work for a San Francisco company called Computer Hand Holding, Inc., and as the name implies, technical support is our primary product. Founded by my friend Emil Flock in 1983, Computer Hand Holding was one of the first companies providing third-party support services for a variety of clients. Some of those clients are hardware and software manufacturers who rely on us to help their customers. Others are organizations that contract with us to help their employees with a variety of products. To date, we've taken over 100,000 calls for both of these types of clients, and I've taken a few thousand of those myself. As training and information systems manager, I've also had a chance to help our new employees learn the ropes and give them some of the tools they need to do the job better.

Since I work for a third-party support organization, my company is probably different than yours, but I hope, nonetheless, to speak to your concerns. Since I do support for both manufacturers and end-user organizations, I'm able to address the important issues for both types of support. I've supplemented my own experience by seeking out a number of insiders to add their insights into different aspects of support.

I've looked at support from a number of angles, but my starting point has been my own experience in providing it. Tech support is no simple job. It can be tough, rewarding, and frustrating, and it's always highly educational. It's never the same two days in a row, or two calls in a row, and it never feels like you've quite mastered it. It's hard to say what's more challenging—dealing with the technology or the folks you try to help. In my experience, the vast majority of those people have been patient, friendly, and appreciative, though a few have been so nasty that I still shudder to think about their calls. I hope none of the latter type ever call you, but I have included some tips for handling them if they ever do.

Recommended Reading

This book is one of very few on computer technical support. There are quite a number, however, on the subject of customer service in general, and the importance of service both inside a business and outside.

If "quality" was the watchword of the eighties, a number of influential business writers have spoken of the 1990s as the decade of service. They argue that businesses will be forced to offer better customer service in order to survive and prosper in an increasingly competitive world economy. Since technical support is very much part of customer service, we ought to become familiar with some of these key thinkers of the "service revolution." After all, they're allies in our efforts to improve the status and resources of the profession.

Total Customer Service

One of the hottest business books of 1989 was *Total Customer Service,* written by William H. Davidow and Bro Uttal (Harper & Row, 1989). Davidow had worked at Hewlett-Packard and Intel and makes a number of references to computer product support, but this book has a more general focus.

The authors maintain that business in general is doing a pretty lousy job in customer service, and their view is that the situation is getting worse. They cite a number of causes of the current crisis, including the following.

- Exclusive focus on short term profits

- Technology that's increasingly complex, prone to problems, and hard to support

- Rising expectations on the part of consumers

Most managers, according to Davidow and Uttal, don't have a clue about what to do about the service crisis. They often fail to realize they have a problem because they focus on misleading indicators such as the number of customer complaints. Unfortunately, only a small minority of customers (two to four percent, according to one study) ever bother to complain because they don't expect anything to get better. Instead they spread their negative judgments about products to all their friends.

Even worse, Davidow and Uttal say, is the tendency of management to define service in narrow terms. Management fails to perceive strategic opportunities to get close to the customers. Instead management creates customer service departments to listen politely to complaints without having much power to act on them. I think many support people may recognize themselves in this role, unfortunately.

Much of *Total Customer Service* consists of the authors' six-point plan for beating the lousy service syndrome, which I can only sketch briefly here.

- Develop a service strategy. Segment customers into groups with like expectations and target each group appropriately. Influence customer expectations so that you can surpass them.

- Foster service leadership. Create a service culture, and make sure service is everybody's business. Keep bureaucracy from strangling service.

- Motivate and train employees. People who talk to customers have traditionally had low status and minimal training. That has to be changed.

- Make more serviceable products. Prevent complaints by doing better design and testing.

- Invest in service infrastructure. Use technology to get a handle on service demand and keep investing in it to stay ahead of the game.

- Monitor achievement of service goals. Find appropriate measures of how customers are being served. Reward achievement of your service goals.

Many of these ideas are reflected in later chapters of *Help!*, but I recommend *Total Customer Service* to anyone trying to make support work better, especially those who work for computer product manufacturers. Though I believe their scathing assessment of service quality is only partially applicable to the computer industry, Davidow and Uttal have a lot of good ideas about how to make it better.

. . . .

Service Without and Within

Another customer service guru worth studying is Karl Albrecht. He's written and cowritten a number of popular books including *Service America!* (Dow Jones-Irwin, 1985), *At America's Service* (Dow Jones-Irwin, 1988), and *The Service Advantage* (Dow Jones-Irwin, 1989).

One of Albrecht's key ideas is "the moment of truth," which he defines as "any episode in which the customer comes into contact with any aspect of the organization and gets an impression of the quality of the service." A business imperative, according to Albrecht, should be to make sure that every one of these moments, from product ads, to packaging, to design, to after-sales service, meets or exceeds the customer's expectations.

Of course, some moments are more important than others, and these require "special care and feeding," according to Albrecht. To bring the concept back to technical support, the moment when a computer user finds himself unable to get work done due to a bug or misunderstanding would seem to be just such a moment. That user is likely to make lasting judgments about the quality of service he gets when he calls for help.

In a new book, *Service Within* (Dow Jones-Irwin, 1990), Albrecht brings his service gospel to the arena of service *within* organizations. Albrecht says relations between departments are frequently bureaucratic and unproductive. One key to making things better, he says, is finding ways to revitalize the role and outlook of middle management, but he also offers a number of other suggestions for improving internal service that computer support people in information centers and help desks can make use of, a few of which I list here.

- Figure out who your customers are. Albrecht suggests imagining who would complain if you stopped doing your job for a while.

- Identify and analyze your moments of truth. Investigate how well your customers think you're handling those moments.

. . . .

- Focus on contributions your department can make to the overall organization instead of on its formal functions.

- Recognize that your department may have dual missions of service and policing. Strive to make those missions compatible.

- Develop a comprehensive service mission statement, tie it to a concrete service plan, and get the word out about it.

Ideas and Inspiration

Support professionals should find inspiration and good ideas in these books. Managers need a little theory to help them see the forest (instead of just the trees) and a little ammunition in the battle for resources. And if your job is answering phones instead of making management policy, you'll still benefit from looking at the big picture. Besides, who knows where you'll be a few years from now?

The Shape of This Book

Each of the chapters in this book is self-contained, and you may read them in any order. To help you find what's most interesting to you, here's a brief description of each chapter.

In Chapter 1, *Manufacturer Support,* I focus on the management of technical support departments in hardware and software companies. I look at the importance of support to manufacturers and how customers assess the quality of the support they're currently getting. The chapter covers the economics of support, and presents the continuing debate over whether support should be fee-based or included in the price of the product. I also look at some of the key "people issues," such as what companies can do to attract, train, and keep good people in jobs that are often stressful and demanding. I also suggest some things that managers should do to measure and set service levels and to sell the importance of support both inside and outside the company.

Chapter 2, *Internal Support,* also covers management issues, but this time the arena is the inhouse support operation, the help desks corporations and other organizations have put in place to aid their employees in using computers. What is the primary mission of the help desk, and how should it view the people it serves? What can internal support do to meet the challenges of increased technical complexity, decreased resources, staff burnout, and varied user needs? I also look at alternatives to the traditional help desk such as peer support and third-party services, as well as efforts to bring support to the world of non-profit organizations.

With Chapter 3, *Communication Skills,* we turn to the question of what support professionals can do to communicate effectively with the people who call for help. I maintain that communication can be improved just like other skills, and in this chapter we take a very practical approach to the interpersonal challenges support people routinely face. How do you create rapport with callers, listen effectively to their questions and problems, convey a convincing authority with your voice and words, and deliver your technical explanations in language appropriate to the caller? I also deal with tough issues like how to deal with angry and abusive callers and those who talk on forever.

Chapter 4, *Handling Support Calls,* continues the practical approach to improving support effectiveness, but here I discuss techniques to deal with the content of the technical support call itself. Classifying calls into a number of basic types, including customer service, feedback, questions, and problems, I offer suggestions about how each can be efficiently handled. In the section on handling problems, I offer a detailed discussion of troubleshooting techniques that usually help in solving the tough ones as quickly as possible.

Chapter 5, *Information Techniques and Tools,* the subject is how to gather, organize, and make available the technical information that's vital to providing quality support. Without effective information techniques, the support organization is crippled, as the same questions get researched over and over and new employees have to learn what the issues are the hard way—on the phone. I look at what information has to be recorded and on ways to organize it, as well as at new technologies like hypertext and expert systems that show promise in helping people give better support.

Finally, I look at some commercial products currently available to help solve support's information challenge.

In Chapter 6, *Alternative Methods of Support,* the focus is on ways to help users that go beyond the traditional support hotline. The chapter looks at some relatively new approaches, including bulletin board support, fax, technical knowledgebases, and remote control software. We'll hear from support professionals who use these technologies regularly to help users, in many cases more economically and efficiently than is possible with the traditional telephone support call.

Chapter 7, *A User's Guide to Tech Support,* takes a look at the support business from a different point of view, the user's. The idea is to get support professionals thinking about what users experience when they need help, as well as to help professionals get better service when they're on the other side of the phone. I'll offer some suggestions about such subjects as how to evaluate products with regard to support, how to avoid unnecessary calls for help, and how to get through on clogged support lines when you really need to. Then I'll discuss ways callers can communicate better with support staff, how to make sure your problem doesn't "fall through the cracks," and how to complain when you feel you haven't gotten the support you deserve.

Finally, an appendix, *Support Resources,* lists a number of organizations that are working for better support.

As the process of writing this book reaches completion, I'm well aware that there are subjects not covered here that could have been. Telephone technology, for example, is important to a support operation but it's not a subject I felt qualified to tackle. Making choices about what to include and what to leave out, I've discovered, is the hardest part of writing a book like this.

. . . .

Acknowledgements

I received a lot of support in writing this book, for which I'm deeply grateful. First of all, I thank the people who generously shared their time and professional experience. Some of them are not quoted directly here, but they helped shape the book nonetheless. My colleagues at Computer Hand Holding, led by Emil Flock and Mike Corse, offered many good ideas and much patience. Ted Nace, my publisher, gave his enthusiasm and trust and then supplied me with the most skillful and supportive editors an author could hope for, Susie Hammond and Steve Roth of Open House. They were ably assisted by sharp-eyed copyeditor Rebecca Wilkinson-Nickell and production director Don Sellers. Artist Mari Stein took my vague and contradictory ideas, added her imagination and skill, and produced the illustrations.

Finally, my deepest thanks to Marilyn Curry, my wife, for encouraging me to start the book and to finish it, and providing loving sustenance in between.

Your Support

Whether you're a beginner or an old pro, I'd appreciate your ideas, reactions, and suggestions regarding this book for future editions. Please send them to me care of my publisher.

Ralph Wilson

Contents

CHAPTER 2

Internal Support

. . . .

CHAPTER 5

Information Techniques and Tools

137

. . . .

CHAPTER 6

Alternative Methods of Support

173

CHAPTER 7

A User's Guide to Tech Support

197

Help!

Manufacturer Support

Creating great technology is tough. So is convincing people to buy it. But once your product's out the door the fun's just beginning—you've got to support it! That means dealing with people who barely know how to plug in a computer, let alone use one, or who bought your product to do something it was never designed for. Other folks will want to tell you how to improve your product, or where you can put it. Of course, you'll also have to deal with conflicts with other products you've never heard of. And, every now and again, you've got to deal with bugs, documentation errors, and other minor shortcomings of your nearly perfect product.

In this chapter we consider support inside hardware and software manufacturers, looking at how it's being done and how to do it better. We'll consider some recent survey data about support in the microcomputer software industry and listen to some leading executives and observers talk about such issues as support's strategic importance, its costs, how to find and foster good people, the uses of technology, and how support fits into the high technology company. I highlight key issues such as whether support should be free to the customer or fee-based and how to sell the importance of support to upper management and others.

....

Current Perceptions

Manufacturer support has taken heat from computer users and the press for a long time. Here are some excerpts from an article that's only slightly more outspoken than most in its assessment.

> Picking up the phone to call a customer support line can be like playing Russian roulette. Sometimes you can walk away without a scratch, but other times you walk away mortally wounded, or at least confused, frustrated, and angry.
>
> Sometimes it seems a miracle that any questions get answered in the world of tech support, where frustrated users meet harried customer support staff on a battlefield of complex technology.
>
> Telephone calls go unanswered; floppy disks get lost in the mail; different service technicians give different answers to the same question; and sometimes—if you're lucky—you get the right answer the first time. (*PC Week*, Nov. 14, 1988.)

More recent comments by well-known computer journalist Jim Seymour indicate that the support offered by hardware and software manufacturers has been improving.

> In my experience, the quality of telephone support from most vendors has gone up dramatically over the last two years. And I find the level of training and courtesy among tech support people much better today than in years past. (*PC Magazine*, Apr. 24, 1990.)

Although Seymour's positive comments came in the middle of an essay lamenting "that product development and after-sale support are so far out of sync today," the positive changes he notes may reflect manufacturers' increased emphasis on support and a realization that users are increasingly sophisticated and demanding. Companies are discovering that quality of support is a key factor in the purchase decisions of many customers.

Despite the occasional horror story, there are signs that customers are generally pretty satisfied with the support manufacturers are providing today. A recent survey by *PC World* (Oct. 1990) reported that 60 percent of its readers surveyed rated hardware and software support as good or excellent. Only a small proportion rated current support as unsatisfactory—seven percent for software, 10 percent for hardware.

The Importance of Support

Support, as we'll see, is a significant cost of doing business, so the first question to ask is why offer support at all? What's the role of support in the business strategies of hardware and software companies?

Writing in the *WPCorp Report* (Oct. 1988), WordPerfect vice president of marketing M. Daniel Lunt wrote that his company has "a moral responsibility" to support its products, and that there are important subsidiary benefits that justify the high expense. "If we have no obligation to support our products, we have less motivation to produce products that are trouble free."

Eric Ornas, manager of customer support of Borland International, describes the strategic value of high-quality support in dealing with more entrenched competition.

> It offers you some great leverage. It's typical of selling any product, it's the value added. The other person is maybe more established but you're going to do business with me, because I'm going to give you not only this and that, but I'm going to add these other things. Support is a great sales tool.
>
> There is such a proliferation of products, it's dizzying. People need to have a connection with the company that they're going to work with, but even before they make that connection they need to develop a sense that the company is going to stand by them, because they're hanging their business on this product. If you can give them access to the information they need, that gives you a leg up.

Support has another role to play, less exalted perhaps than creating good will, less exciting than providing a competitive advantage, but vital. Here's Deborah Fain, a fifteen-year veteran in the support business. She co-founded the Samna Corporation and later MSR, a third-party support company. Currently, she is president of Lysis Corporation, a producer of support software.

It's unfortunate, but software companies—and I'm sure hardware too—because of marketing conditions or whatever, are often forced into releasing product before it should ever be released; the test cycle will be five days when it really should be three months. Consequently, the people that make it possible for that product to stay installed are tech support. Without that support, the customers would just send it back. As a result most high technology companies rely very heavily on support, although they can't tell you the value of it. They know instinctively that if they don't have it they're not going to have users, and I think we'll see that even more as the industry matures and gets more competitive.

Support will typically calm the customers down, find a workaround, ensure that they'll be updated—all those things that you can't do with a book and you can't afford to do with an onsite person. Support does all that, and we all know of products that people kept just because we told them it was going to be okay, and they trusted us.

Relying on Dealers Given these reasons to provide support, it may seem surprising that some of the major players in the microcomputer industry choose not to provide technical support to customers at all, at least not directly. Buy a new computer from some of the largest companies and you won't have direct access to those companies' tech support departments; rather, you'll be referred to your dealer for support.

Many hardware manufacturers want to avoid "throwing bodies" and lots of money at the problems of support, especially since their customers number in the millions. Up to now, lack of direct support hasn't kept those millions from buying from those highly reputed big manufacturers.

Whether dealers have the resources to provide the same service as a manufacturer's internal tech support department depends on many factors, but most of them come down to money. As Charles Humphrey wrote in *PC Week* (Apr. 30, 1990), the retail distribution channel "has no war chest with which to invest in support. It has scraped by on razor-thin margins for years, and whatever was left was depleted in last year's price wars." Where will the cash come from to train and inform sales people so that they can answer their customers questions?

A survey conducted by *Computer Reseller News* (July 16, 1990) found the average computer salesperson received only 6.3 days of training in 1989. That's hardly enough to qualify them to support customers with tough problems. Some manufacturers do back up resellers with extensive training, and many provide access to high quality dealer support hotlines and electronic bulletin boards. I won't be able to cover tech support in the retail channel any further here, except to say that some dealers are heroic in finding solutions to their customers' problems, whereas others have little to offer after the sale. Customers seem to prefer having the option of manufacturer-supplied tech support. *PC World* (Oct. 1990) reported a survey of 1,000 readers who gave dealer support lower marks overall than manufacturers.

Support Economics

The people who run computer software and hardware companies are in business to make money, whatever fascination they have with technology and whatever desires they might have to offer service to their customers. In this section we'll investigate the economics of support and the hotly debated issue of who pays for it and how.

Information about economic issues in support is much easier to come by for software than for hardware manufacturers, so the emphasis of this section is on the former. I'd prefer more balanced coverage, but this emphasis does reflect the fact that when it comes to PC hardware, support is largely focused on repair and maintenance issues, rather than user assistance, the subject of this book. The picture seems to be changing, though, with several hardware makers offering high-profile, high-quality hotline support, in some cases 24 hours a day, 365 days a year. If the trend continues, there will doubtless be lots of information about hardware support economics in the future, but for the present, we'll have to assume that the numbers are similar to those for software companies, although some of the largest hardware manufacturers provide support only through the retail channel.

When it comes to software support economics, survey research by *Soft•Letter* of Watertown, Massachusetts is a valuable resource. In February 1990, *Soft•Letter*, a newsletter covering "trends and strategies in software publishing," published what may be the most thorough survey ever conducted of the technical support practices, policies, and experience of microcomputer software publishers in the United States.

Based on voluntary responses from 282 companies, the survey provides a bench mark of the current state of user support within the software industry. Manufacturers surveyed produce software for DOS, Macintosh, UNIX, OS/2, Apple II, Atari, and Amiga platforms. Most of the companies produce software for more than one platform. Only independent software manufacturers (not associated with computer manufacturers) were included in the survey. The median installed base for the companies' was 12,000, with the 50 percent range extending from 2,000 to 80,000 copies.

Though respondents included both large and small companies, a large number, 42 percent, were in the smallest category, those with less than $1 million in sales. Forty-one percent had sales of $1 to $10 million and 17 percent sold more than $10 million. The median support center head count for these small companies was two (50 percent range 2-8). Companies with sales from $1 to $10 million averaged four support employees (50 percent range 3-8) and those selling more than $10 million had a median of 20 (50 percent range 10-31). The "mega" support centers of the largest software houses, like WordPerfect's or Microsoft's with several hundred employees each, are clearly "off the scale" of this survey data. The vast majority of support operations are on a much more modest scale.

How Much Do They Spend on Support?

When *Soft•Letter* asked microcomputer software companies how much they spent on total support costs as a percentage of net sales, the median response was 6 percent, with the 50 percent range extending from 3.25 percent to 11 percent. *Soft•Letter* found only a small difference between median expenditures on different platforms. For example, Mac software companies reported a 5 percent median, DOS companies 6 percent, and UNIX houses 7 percent.

What do these figures really mean? What do software companies spend on other things? To put these figures in perspective let's look at the operating ratios of microcomputer software companies reported in *Soft•Letter*'s 1989 annual report on the microcomputer software industry—figures which give a yardstick against which to compare support expenditures. According to that report, sales and marketing accounted for 30 percent of income, general and administration 20 percent, cost of goods sold 18 percent, research and development 10 percent. This left profit of 22 percent.

Support expenditures of 6 percent don't seem to be extraordinarily large to the context of such numbers, though shaving a couple of percent would no doubt make stockholders happy, assuming those points ended up on the profit side of the ledger. On the other hand, it might be wise to take these figures for overall support expenditures with a few grains of salt. Support veteran and software entrepreneur Deborah Fain of Lysis Corporation in Decatur, Georgia, had this to say when I asked about the numbers.

I don't think they have the foggiest notion what they're spending on support. That's what WordPerfect allocates, so that's what everyone says they're doing, in my opinion. I think it depends on the level of support you want to be giving, and everyone is just sort of decided on that figure.

Eric Ornas of Borland points out that it's difficult to compare expenditures on support by different companies.

We all measure things differently. We don't all roll up the same kinds of costs into that overall technical service number. And until we standardize, it doesn't mean a whole lot to say that it costs one company this and another company something else. In spite of that, we're trying to look at that number, but we haven't agreed on what should be included in it.

Whose Nickel? Most companies expect their customers to pay for the phone call to their hotlines. A substantial minority of 28 percent offers toll-free 800 number support for their products and another 8 percent plans to add 800 service. Many companies find toll-free service prohibitive, both because of the immediate cost—$1 to $2 per call—and the increased call volumes free access might encourage. One executive was quoted as saying his company wouldn't offer 800 lines because "customers then call without even trying to read the manual."

WordPerfect built its pre-eminent reputation for support around its toll-free lines. Proudly making marketing hay, Word-Perfect once ran a famous ad showing its monthly phone bill, then in the $160,000 range. That bill is now almost $500,000 a month. Stan MacKay, WordPerfect's manager of customer support, says his company considered doing away with its 800 number service in 1987 and joining the majority who let customers put up the nickel.

We were going back and forth, and Pete Peterson, our executive vice president, came back from the Software Publishers Association conference saying very strongly we're not going to question toll-free support, "We've always had that philosophy and we're going to keep it." Part of the reason was everyone else was going toll, and he saw a way to make us unique in the industry by making us un-limited, toll-free support. And it's always worked for us.

To some, toll-free service may be an expensive, but unappreciated frill. Writing in *PC Magazine*, Jim Seymour claims, "Business users couldn't care less whether they have to pay for a support call. It's not *their* money… The cost of the call is simply too small—even when it's multiplied by hundreds or thousands of PC users in a large company—to show up on that company's balance sheet."

Yet many users seem to think otherwise. *PC World*'s readers rated toll-free access as pretty important in a recent survey, 4.2 on a scale of 1 to 5.

The Great Debate: Free or Fee-based Support?

Let's face it, support is never free. Whether users pay an annual fee for access to hotlines or never have to write another check after the initial purchase, the cost of providing postsales support has to come from customers somehow. For simplicity, though, I'll refer to support that customers receive without having to pay a fee beyond the product's purchase price as "free." Programs that involve direct user payments for support I'll refer to as "fee-based."

Whatever the current breakdown between fee-based and free support, there are clearly pressures building in the software industry to find ways to offset the costs of support. Let's look at some of the key arguments in the raging debate between advocates of the two approaches, starting with three in favor of fee-based support.

The "leaky bucket" argument. To some insiders the need for users to pay directly for support is fundamental, part of the basic economics of the situation. An articulate advocate of this position is Deborah Fain of Lysis Corporation. Ms. Fain makes an analogy to the social security system.

If we think about how many people are paying into Social Security and how many people are taking out of it, eventually we'll get to a point where more people are taking out than are paying in. The same thing happens to anyone who

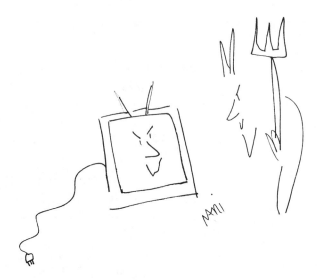

is selling a product and giving support away free forever, because eventually your installed base, which is drawing on your support dollars, is larger than the number of people you can sell to every month who are actually contributing support dollars.

So if we take WordPerfect as the personification of a company that believes in free support forever, so long as its sales are growing at a significant enough rate that the payin exceeds the payout, they're all right. But at some point everyone's sales flatten out. That doesn't mean that you're not still a profitable company, you just don't see the peaks you saw before, and when that happens, every single month your installed base continues to grow, and eventually the money you're paying out is more than you can possibly bring in.

According to Fain, this trend can lead in only one direction. "What happens is that the support begins deteriorating, because you just simply can't afford it if you're going to stay in business."

The "savvy user" argument. This argument focuses on the user, who's seen as increasingly able to go it alone without support.

Why should he be forced to absorb the support costs incurred by novices and people who refuse to open the manual? *PC Magazine*'s Jim Seymour put it succinctly in a recent essay (Sept. 25, 1990).

> When we were all new to PCs, the great majority of customers could be assumed to need 3.5 calls of an average duration of 10.2 minutes each, over the first 3.8 months of use. So spreading the cost of postsale support across *all* customers was both fair and good business. Now though, users are so savvy that many need no telephone support. Others work for companies that provide support internally. Why, the argument goes, should these customers be assessed an upfront charge for support they'll never seek?

The savvy user says, "I do my homework, why should I pay more for a product so that people who don't know what the inside of the manual looks like can get all the help they need?"

The "bottom line" argument. This argument says support must pay its own way if it's ever to get any respect within the corporation. Otherwise, support is condemned to second-class status, viewed as a necessary evil, and forced to eke out a minimal existence. Many support executives believe that they'll only become first-class citizens within the corporation when they can change support from being a cash drain to a cash cow.

A tighter business climate intensifies the pressure. Jim Seymour in the same *PC Magazine* issue as above talks about the bottom line.

> …with margins shrinking in the software business and aggressive price-shopping by almost every software buyer, publishers have every incentive to strip as many costs as possible out of the purchase price, both to compete effectively and to support their sagging gross margins. Support costs are the first, easiest, and most obvious to go.

That 6 percent of net sales average we mentioned earlier may not seem like a lot at first, but when things get tighter, it begins to appear more significant.

Now let's look at the other side, the arguments for providing free support. The advocates of this position are just as profit oriented as the fee-based partisans. They know the cost is high, but they think it's worth it, for hard-nosed, business reasons.

The "good service sells" argument. You offer free support because it shows your customers that you stand behind your product and that you want to help them with it. Customers respond by buying your product. WordPerfect Corporation is the leading example of this position, offering high quality, unlimited support and even making the phone call toll-free. Stan MacKay of WordPerfect says the company's generous support policies have had a clear effect on the bottom line.

> If you take Microsoft Word and WordPerfect, most people have a really hard time determining which is better, because they both have pretty much the same features, keystrokes are close, the way they do things is close. The only difference is the way we support our products, and that's getting credit for the 30 percent market gain last year. So you never put it in numbers, but when you look at the result, it certainly adds to the bottom line.

The "inherent problems" argument. This argument points at the nature of computer products, their complexity, the inevitable presence of bugs, and the shortcomings of documentation. How can you charge a customer several hundred dollars for a product, then charge him again for the privilege of reporting a bug and requesting a fix, or to get an explanation of a manual that is poorly written. When did you last see a sticker as in Figure 1-1 on a computer product?

On the contrary, the growth of the microcomputer industry was built on the premise that ordinary people who don't spend all their time thinking about computers can use these products to get work done. Does charging people for support send the right message?

The "reasonable expense" argument. According to this argument, the demand for tech support is not as overwhelming as

Figure 1-1

> **WARNING!**
> Don't buy this product unless you're an advanced computer user or you're prepared to spend a good deal of time reading a technical manual because it's pretty complicated. And don't expect to get our help with any product malfunctions unless you pay an extra support fee.

it's often depicted, and certainly not so great as to justify the "need" to charge. According to *Soft•Letter*'s support survey, the average software package generates one support call, with the 50 percent range being 0.15 to 2.6 calls. Not exactly a deluge. Further, the survey found that two-thirds of those calls occurred within 90 days of sale. That doesn't leave many calls left to be charged for, since most companies with fee-based plans offer at least a 45 to 90 day initial free period.

The Current Situation: Decidedly Mixed

Despite warnings by the computer press that free support is going the way of the snail darter, the situation is still quite mixed. See Table 1-1. The majority of the software companies surveyed by *Soft•Letter* (60 percent) still offer no fee, bundled support. The percentages vary depending on the company size, with unlimited free support offered by 69 percent of the smallest companies ($1 million or less in sales), 56 percent of the midsize companies ($1–$10 million), and only 53 percent of the largest companies ($10 million+).

Three Ways to Pay

Smaller companies tend to offer free support, perhaps because they feel they must. Many larger ones feel equally compelled to extract revenues from their support departments, using a number of different arrangements. Let's look at three of them.

Free now, pay later. The most common fee-based approach currently is to limit the period of free support (often to 90 days) and make any subsequent calls contingent on the customer paying for an annual support contract. This contract might include a number of incentives, such as toll-free access or one year of free

Table 1-1 Support offerings

	All	< $1MM	$1MM-$10MM	Over $10MM
Unlimited	60%	69%	56%	53%
Limited to period after purchase	13%	12%	13%	15%
Limited to period after first call	4%	2%	4%	9%
Unlimited until next upgrade	2%	4%	0%	2%
Paid only	11%	7%	13%	11%
Other	10%	5%	14%	11%

(Source: *Soft•Letter*)

software upgrades. A high-profile example is Lotus Corporation, which recently began offering six months of free support with its products. During that period, support is toll-free and available 24 hours a day, seven days a week. After those first six months of Rolls Royce service, Lotus hopes users will pay for continued support at the same level.

Premium support plans. Premium plans usually include expedited, front-of-the-queue service, often by more senior support staff. Other incentives being offered include special upgrade privileges, toll-free access, technical information bulletins, and other perks. Some premium plans are targeted at individuals, offer a limited number of calls, and sell for less than $200. Others are aimed at corporations, often including unlimited, toll-free calls, and support people assigned specifically to each account. These plans can cost several thousand dollars a year.

900 numbers. A new wrinkle in the support game is the use of 900 numbers as a form of paid support. Usually 900 numbers are offered as an alternative to a support contract after an initial period of free support, but some companies are positioning them as a way to get expedited, premium service, even when free support is available. Some 900 numbers cost users a couple of dollars a minute. Others charge a flat fee of, say, $15. Customers seem to be fairly open to 900-number support according to early reports from the several companies that have implemented it.

Nine hundred numbers have serious problems, however. Many businesses block their employees from dialing them. It's difficult to credit callers who aren't helped, or who have to call back on the same problem. Another problem is the fact that the phone company takes a sizable cut.

Is Anyone Buying? How are people responding to paid support plans? Not with overwhelming enthusiasm. Thirty-seven percent of new customers and 34 percent of older ones signed up for fee-based support contracts, according to *Soft•Letter*'s survey, and about 64 percent of these renewed after the first year. It may be that users feel they can get most of the help they'll need within the period of free support most companies offer, and they may be right. As we've seen, two-thirds of all calls for help came within 90 days of purchase, and there was an average of one call per package, according to the survey.

Despite the lukewarm response fee-based support plans are getting, a third of the companies that offer them reported to *Soft•Letter* that support contracts made their support operations into significant profit centers for their companies, with the rest reporting support as a "breakeven" proposition (48 percent) or an "unprofitable" (19 percent) operation. Though these numbers may not be overwhelming, it's clear that some companies are beginning to make significant money from support. Ledgeway Group, a Lexington, Massachusetts market research firm specializing in customer service, estimates that fee-based PC software support was a $250,000,000 market in 1989 and expects it to reach $750,000,000 by 1993.

A Big Player Returns to Free Support Interestingly, one of the pioneers in the fee-based support approach among PC software manufacturers, Ashton-Tate, has returned to a policy of unlimited free support for registered owners of its products. Mike Semagran, director of technical support services at Ashton-Tate explains why.

We now have free telephone support, not toll-free—the user pays for the call—but it's free, unlimited support. That is a significant change for Ashton-Tate that occurred at the first of the year. About three years ago Ashton-Tate was the first in the microcomputer industry to start fee-for-service support, and it's not that we're going away from that, but we're changing our approach. We're saying that because there is an expectation in the microcomputer industry for free support we're going to do that too. I call it vanilla support. If you want vanilla, it's free. If your needs are greater than what we provide for free, you're going to pay for it.

Ashton-Tate has returned to free, unlimited hotline support augmented by a variety of electronic support modes that it hopes will relieve its phone lines. It also offers premium, fee-based support plans to the customers who are willing to pay for more deluxe service. Customers' negative response to solely fee-based support seems to have caused the company to rethink it's earlier, exclusively fee-based approach.

What's in Store? Many insiders have predicted the imminent demise of free support, but the obituary is premature. Some of the biggest software makers have begun to limit the amount of free support they offer, and early predictions from insiders were that the rest would soon follow suit. So far that hasn't happened. Instead of a headlong rush we seem to be in a holding pattern. Users haven't leaped at the chance to pay for what they used to get free, or for what they can still get free from a competitor. Some companies are even moving in the other direction, returning to unlimited free support after finding that many customers demand it.

Yet other manufacturers have begun to make a significant amount of money from support fees and the industry is clearly eyeing the possibility of turning an expensive cost item into a profit center. PC pundit Jim Seymour says that the key is targeting the different parts of the user population appropriately. He asserts, "The surge of interest in 900-number, pay-per-call support is both a stalking horse for those annual service agreements and a way of separating customers into business and individual categories. Publishers want to force customers into one group or the other." (*PC Magazine*, Sept. 25, 1990.)

If Seymour is correct, we'll see 900 numbers emerge, despite their problems, as the primary mode for individuals to access support lines. Most individual users call only once or twice shortly after purchase, and they'll find it more palatable to pay $15 for each call than to subscribe to an annual support contract. Corporate users will probably turn first to their own companies' help desks when they're stuck, and those help desks will be signed up for the software companies' premium support plans for backup. Although it's too early to tell whether this scenario will prevail, it's likely that 900 numbers for support will be a growing phenomenon along with other fee-based approaches.

Nonetheless, I believe that free support will continue to be offered by a significant portion of the industry, despite the high cost of providing it. Free support is in keeping with the trend toward service quality and customer focus that's the key to business survival in an increasingly competitive era. Free support sends a powerful positive message to customers and it's been a factor in some of the industry's biggest success stories. The key question is whether companies offering free support will be able to keep their quality up and their hold times down.

Free or Fee, You've Got To Do It Right

Whichever approach you take, free or fee-based support, you've got plenty of challenges ahead to make it work. Companies that opt for fee-based are going to deal with customer resistance. To overcome it, they'll need to do several things right.

- Offer high-quality, low-frustration service. Customers are going to be even more unhappy to wait on hold if they've had to pay for the privilege.

- Offer incentives. Include updates, technical bulletins, or toll-free access. Adding a sweetener to the deal makes it a much easier sale.

- Offer options. Different customers have different budgets and different support needs. Tailor support deals to different types of users.

- Enforce the rules. Customers hate it if they've paid their fee but no one checks.

Companies that continue to offer unlimited free support face plenty of challenges too.

- Keep up quality. Free support doesn't seem like a bargain to your customers if they can't get through, or get the right answers, or if they have to wait on hold forever.

- Strengthen your support infrastructure. To deal with spiraling costs and keep support from breaking the budget you have to invest in information technology and good people.

- Get some mileage. Trumpet the fact that you provide unlimited support on all your ads and product literature. Make it a marketing tool. Within your own company, too, you have to sell the idea that free support sells products.

Managing Calls

When users complain of endless busy signals and hours on hold, they're experiencing the end results of a company's call-handling policies—not enough lines and/or not enough people to handle the demand.

From the vendor's point of view, calls come in in a terribly difficult pattern. Demand is focused on one or two peak periods during the day, and those peaks may be ten or more times heavier than other times. Staffing to meet the peaks tolerably well without breaking the budget or being overstaffed the rest of the day is a big part of the art of managing support.

Counting the Beans: Measuring Support Center Service Levels

Tech support centers take calls. Whether they come in on the most sophisticated automatic call distributor or a single line phone, calls are the common denominator of vendor support operations, the basic units of measure. As in any business, if you can't measure it, you can't manage it, and you can't know or prove that you're doing a good job.

I sought out 20-year support veteran Bill Rose for his ideas on the fundamentals of managing a support center, the process of setting and maintaining adequate service levels. Rose is a San Diego-based consultant on both manufacturer and internal support operations. His experience includes managing Candle

Corporation's renowned support center, as well as founding the Software Support Professionals Association, a San Diego, California-based forum for support managers. Rose prefaced his remarks on service levels by listing his three rules of software support, noting, "I've seen very few people able to accomplish these three things effectively."

> The first rule is to pick up the phone. It's that simple, yet I still call software vendors and I cannot get through on their telephones, or if I get through I'm on hold forever.
>
> The second rule is to get the customer to the right person. That shouldn't be so difficult. I don't want to talk to an administrative person, I want to talk to a technical person. I don't want to talk to any technical person, I want to talk to a specialist about this particular problem. And I don't want to go on hold forever, and I don't want you to give me a call back.
>
> Rule number three is to count the beans. When I ask a support manager, "How many calls did you take between 10 A.M. and 12 P.M. on June 30, 1985?" he should be able to tell me. He should be able to look back and say, "That's how many calls we took," because that's the most important part of the entire business.

These three fundamentals have to be in place before you can do anything to establish service levels, according to Rose. Without them, any statistical analysis or modelling you do will be meaningless. Once you're achieving the basics, you can begin to measure your present service levels and develop targets for the future.

Rose divides service levels into two basic categories—response time and resolve time. Response time is simply the "pick-up-the-phone" type of thing, the time it takes to get a caller talking to someone who can help. Resolve time is the time it takes to fix the caller's problem or answer his question. Rose says that when it comes to keeping your customers happy, the first priority is to improve response time.

> Doing things to improve response time will buy you more than any other changes you put into software support. We

know from customer satisfaction surveys that the number one issue for customers is the responsiveness of their vendors. If there's a problem, they want to be able to get through to you right away. They don't want to wait, they don't want a call back, they don't want to be put on hold for long periods of time. So service levels should be focused around that issue. We pick up the phone in three rings, or 90 percent of all calls get to level one support on the first callin, or we call everybody back within 24 hours.

Rose makes clear that you can't achieve improvements in satisfaction by putting people on the phones to take messages, which would violate his second support rule, "Get the caller to the right person."

When it comes to the second part of the service equation, resolve time, how long it takes to fix the customer's problem to his satisfaction, support faces some tough challenges.

We have some dilemmas in software support in this area. One of them is that when a customer calls in and says, "Every time I do this, this problem happens," we tell them, "Don't do that!" The customer says, "Thanks."

We call that a circumvention, or a workaround, or a temporary fix. And then we have a problem that goes on some stack somewhere that's waiting to be resolved. But it's not hot anymore. It's low priority, the customer's not doing it anymore, they're working with limited capabilities.

We would never do that with hardware. We'd go out and fix the problem. Yet in software we give them workarounds and it cripples us, because now we have a backlog and we have to deal with that in our resolve time, and we also have to give the customer the status.

Rose says just dealing with the backlog can be a big problem. "On average, 60 percent of the calls that come to a support center are to check status of existing problems. Sometimes it's greater than that." Often the resolution of the problem is outside of the control of the support department, requiring major engineering resources in other departments. The upshot is, don't make promises you can't keep.

You want to be extra careful about committing to resolve times. I see vendors that say, "All problems will be resolved within 48 hours." That's dangerous! You just never know what's going to happen. It could be that from a manpower standpoint you just don't have somebody to work on it.

Rose recommends a different approach, one that combines elements of response time with resolve time.

I try to take what sounds like resolve time but in reality it's response time that we're actually working with. I might say something like, "One hundred percent of all hot calls will be handled immediately." Now "handled" is really a response-type thing. We're telling customers if you have a real hot problem, we're not going to let you off the phone. We'll work with you until we can at least provide a workaround. We're going to get that issue resolved for you. We're not going to say, "We know your system's down, call us tomorrow." We'll work with you immediately.

Rose says that when you seek to improve response time and resolve time, you have to remember that everyone in the organization who deals with customers has a role to play, though their involvement in the two components varies. "The folks in the front end may have less responsibility to resolve but more to be responsive, whereas those in the back end may have more responsibility to resolve and the responsiveness may not be so important." You need to work with each member of the team, setting goals for them to achieve to help meet your overall service level targets. Goals for front-line people, such as "answer the phone within three rings," will be focused on response time. People whose primary task is to resolve problems will have goals like "report problem status to the caller within 24 hours."

Bill Rose's down to earth approach to "counting the beans" is a refreshing alternative to the statistical overkill that management is prone to these days. It's good to keep support in perspective.

We're basically here to answer the phone and solve the problem, and that's what we should keep track of. More of Rose's insights into the support game are presented in his book, *Managing Software Support* (Software Support Professionals Association, 1990).

People Issues

Tech support is a highly labor-intensive operation, regardless of how much companies invest in technology to make it more efficient. Calls have to be handled one by one, by support analysts, technicians, engineers—the term varies. These people have to be knowledgeable in technical and policy matters, as well as have the communication skills to help customers and represent their companies well. Naturally, much of any support manager's time is spent wrestling with issues like figuring staffing requirements, recruitment, training, performance review, and responding to peoples' problems.

Support centers are notorious for producing stress. Technicians are on the firing line, dealing with problem after problem and users who are often confused, frustrated, and angry. The products are never perfect—sometimes by a long shot. And there are invariably times when finding a solution is difficult or impossible. If difficult problems are stressful, so is the repetition of routine questions that are usually a high percentage of all calls. No wonder that whenever support managers meet they're always talking about how to find good people and how to keep them from burning out.

Yet some companies seem to be dealing pretty successfully with these issues. *Soft•Letter*'s survey of software companies found that 63 percent of support technicians stayed on the job at least two years. Interestingly, small companies (under $1 million in sales) managed to keep 81 percent of their support staff for that long as opposed to the biggest ones (over $10 million) who only managed to retain 39 percent. In "Finding and Training Good People" we will look at some of the issues that managers face in managing the human resource.

Finding and Training Good People

At Computer Hand Holding we've been lucky. As a small company we've been able to add staff slowly, relying on newspaper ads and referrals to fill vacancies as they come up. Ads have generated ample replies, and we've often been able to choose among a number of strong candidates (not that we haven't picked a couple of lemons along the way). We've managed to keep people, too. The upshot is that we haven't been exposed to the struggles frequently reported by many managers to staff our support line with qualified people

To find out more about how other companies recruit, hire, and train good people, I contacted the folks at AnswerSet Corporation, a Cupertino, California, company that's recruited staff for dozens of large and small support operations. The people at AnswerSet are support veterans themselves with plenty of experience managing and working in support centers. Led by it's president, Pam Yocum and senior account manager Mary Tasto, AnswerSet's staff shared the job of answering my questions.

Qualifications. These recruiting specialists say it's a never ending challenge to find "that rare breed of person who enjoys working with people, often for long hours on the phone, and who has the technical expertise as well." The difficulty a particular company experiences is usually directly related to the level of expertise required. Naturally enough, the more technical background demanded, and the more complex the product, the harder it is to fill the positions.

Companies' willingness to train new employees also affects the level of expertise required in a candidate, of course. But certain basic qualifications are almost universal.

They need to know and understand the platforms the programs are running on, or in the case of hardware products, have used similar products. They need to exhibit curiosity about computers and the software, and have the ability to learn new applications, languages, etc., very quickly.

Beyond the technical basics, AnswerSet emphasizes that communications skills are usually "*the* most important skill a candidate must have." Adding that since support people must explain technical matters to all levels of users, "they must be good teachers as well as good communicators." In addition there's a broader kind of knowledge about the context in which the tools you're supporting are being used.

Usually, the more a person knows about his area of expertise, and the computing industry over all, the better support person he will be. Many times a customer will say, "This problem is like what happened when I was using this other product." Finding another point of reference when working with a customer can often be very useful. The best support person usually assimilates all he has learned and draws on this knowledge, often unconsciously, to give complete, informed, and rapid answers to a customer.

Training. When it comes to training, most companies seem to take an informal approach, though according to AnswerSet, some larger ones that are constantly hiring new people are starting to develop formal classes to provide consistent training.

The most typical training is either one on one with a seasoned tech support person, or new employees are given a manual, a computer, a phone and told to learn the software on the fly. Often a new tech support person will start with answering letters and faxes, and then progress to call backs only, before taking calls live.

Training can vary from as little as three days to as much as several months, depending on the complexity of the hardware and software to be supported. The average time before a person is ready for full time phone work is probably four weeks. Most people have some time off the phone each week, which they can use to learn new products, along with all the research they have to do on existing products.

The relatively informal approach to training that's common today may not be good enough, with negative results for the customer and heavy demands on the abilities of the support person to master the products under fire.

Tech support people are going to get trained one way or another. They will either get trained at the expense of the customer, or as the result of a formal training program. Since there are few formal training programs, it works only because the support rep, as a general rule, is extremely fast at assimilating information.

The folks at AnswerSet see a trend toward more thorough training as companies realize the negative effects of not offering it. However, they also note pressures within some of the big companies that are constantly adding new staff to get people on the phones prematurely to cope with heavy call volumes. The end result is often dissatisfied customers and frustrated employees.

Salaries. AnswerSet gave the salary ranges shown in Table 1-2 as typical today in Silicon Valley for different levels of experience.

Table 1-2 Salary ranges
1991 - CALIFORNIA

Employed	$
Less than one year	$25–28,000
One to two years	$28–32,000
Two years and above	$30–35,000

They added that UNIX and LAN people would start at $30,000 and go to $50,000, as would those knowledgeable on other complex products. AnswerSet says salaries are continuing to climb, making support a career with a future.

For many people, an entry level position in technical support is a good place to start. For the level of knowledge and expertise required it is often hard to keep people unless the salary increases quickly as their expertise increases.

Managing Support Productivity

Once you've found and hired them, trained them, and put them on the phones, how do you help support people do good work? How do you judge their productivity? I talked to Eric Ornas, an articulate speaker on these subjects from Borland International, about how he and his company have managed to keep people, and keep them happy and productive. When we spoke, Ornas managed a support staff of about 70 support engineers and supervisors as well as Borland's customer service staff. Taking between 1,500 to 2,000 calls a day and growing quickly, Borland is continuously recruiting people to support its business applications and programming languages.

Ornas has spent time on the phones himself, which helps explain his sensitivity to the needs of support people. He told me he talked himself into his first tech support job at MicroPro (now WordStar Corporation) in 1983 despite the fact that he was "a rank beginner." He liked the work and stuck with it, realizing even then that "this was going to get very big."

Time on and off the phones. I first asked Ornas what he felt was a reasonable amount of time for support people to spend on the phones each day.

> Generally, I think five hours is the maximum you want people on the lines. In an eight hour day, five of them can be spent dealing with the customer, and then you need time for training, you need time for research on problems, you need time to stimulate yourself. I think there are limits to how much human contact anyone can have in a day. I also think there's a limit to how sharp you can be, and if you're maxing out, doing the absolute maximum per day, I think you lose that sharpness. So five hours a day and the rest is spent on training, research, projects that help develop the depth that you need.

Of course, there are times when you can't keep to that five hours maximum, like when a flu bug comes to town taking out half the staff, or a new release brings a temporary flood tide of calls. Ornas says support people can step up to handle those emergencies "as long as that's not the *modus operandi*. That wears people out quickly."

The next obvious question is how many calls you can expect people to handle in that five hours on the phone.

> It varies by product, but it doesn't vary all that much. I would say that a reasonable number would be 35 per day. That would be the base line. You have to sort of play down numbers because sometimes people will give you what they think you want, even if they're capable of more. But I've found that's a good baseline for us, though we have people who are doing more than that. It fluctuates

because of the types of calls that you get in a day, but we're comfortable with 35.

Ornas's numbers are in keeping with my own experience and similar to those I've heard from some other managers of high volume support operations, though some push for much higher numbers. Thirty-five calls can be a pretty heavy day's work, but if you have those three hours off the phones, it's a manageable workload. I've found that after 35 calls, I start to feel a little punchy, don't do my best work, and am more likely to have problems with callers.

Evaluation. I asked Ornas what factors he considers when he's evaluating a support person, and he made clear that the raw numbers of calls taken are not the whole story.

> You look at productivity, you look at calls per day, you look at talk time, but you look at it in relation to the rest of the group so you have some basis for comparison. If a person's talk time is consistently higher than everyone else's, for example, or consistently lower, you examine why. Is it a training issue, where this person doesn't have the information? They don't know how to do the troubleshooting in a concise fashion so it's wasting their time and the customer's? Or are they just too conversational, is it really the communication style? For lower talk times you look to see whether these people have the secret of the good call, or if they're not giving the service that the customers require. In addition to just looking at the numbers, the management team has to work with the individual support engineer.

I next asked Ornas about the sensitive subject of monitoring, listening in on calls to evaluate the quality of the support person's work. He does do side-by-side monitoring, listening in on calls with the support person's knowledge, and feels that it serves a number of important purposes.

> One, obviously, you check to make sure that people are handling people the way they should. And you also learn a

lot about the customer if you're not talking to them daily. For example, I can no longer get on and support Borland products and I'll get far away from the customer if I'm not listening. So I will listen to calls with an engineer while the engineer is talking to one of them.

Monitoring isn't a punitive, we're-spying-on-you kind of thing. It's how management really learns what the issues are, what are the engineers dealing with every day. Because by the time I get a customer, they're talking to me on a different level. For example, if you get a screamer, by the time they get to me they might be very nice, very calm, very reasonable, but when they got in they really ripped into the engineer. You get an insight into the issues for the customers, their attitudes. It's just a great training tool.

Just as when discussing other aspects of staff evaluation, Ornas emphasizes the use of monitoring to aid learning, both for management and staff, rather than as a tool to squeeze the last ounce of productivity out of employees. That might be one reason that Borland has had a lot of success retaining its highly trained support people.

Career path. Another factor in employee retention at Borland is offering a viable career path within the organization.

We're putting in a structure that allows growth within the department, and not just in a managerial vein, so that good senior people can stay in tech support longer. Too often, if you want to grow within an organization you have to eventually go into management. We're always working on getting our tech support people more tied in with the company, working on projects on a regular basis. That's important because when people work only with the customer that wears them out. There's no question about it.

Naturally, Borland's policy of encouraging support people to work with other parts of the company can mean that you lose some of them to those other departments, but Ornas is sure this can be a positive factor for support as well.

We have former technical support people now in product management, research and development, quality assurance, field engineering. We're actively promoting that. I think that's the key to two things—getting good people and keeping them. Giving them the opportunity to move on. When you make those opportunities available there's less of a drive to get out. And it's a hell of a recruiting tool, to be able to say that you have moved people through your organization.

Ornas sees tech support maturing, beginning to become "a viable long-term career objective for people. Right now I think it's not often perceived that way." If that positive change is taking place, some of the credit will be to managers like Eric Ornas who have a commitment to the field and the people who take the calls.

Dealing with Stress and Burnout

One of the tough challenges of any service profession is stress. Support is certainly no exception, and many managers are well aware of the danger that their best people will one day hang up their headsets and walk out, vowing never to deal with another rude caller or buggy product again. Let's look at some of the aspects of the work that can cause high stress.

Emotional labor. Management guru Karl Albrecht uses this term to describe the difficult interpersonal component of customer service work. You deal with a stream of different people all day with little control of the work flow. You have to use your own feelings in the work, responding with empathy and understanding to the customer whether he's angry, frustrated, or confused. The folks at AnswerSet put it succinctly, "Technical support people have to be always 'on' when they are dealing with the customers—pleasant, knowledgeable, diplomatic." Not many people can do this kind of work indefinitely without suffering stress. Many choose to get out of direct customer contact work as soon as the opportunity comes along.

Mental labor. Support work presents tough intellectual challenges as well as emotional ones. You're usually trying to solve tough problems without even being able to see the equipment. You must rely on callers who may or may not be able to tell you what's going on, or to carry out your instructions reliably. As AnswerSet says, it can be like "going to all day job interviews day after day, where your technical expertise is under constant scrutiny." Having to concentrate and stay focused for long stretches can leave you drained.

Undervalued labor. Many support people don't get a sense that they're appreciated or listened to. The support veterans at AnswerSet put it clearly.

> Within many companies support is looked upon as a necessary evil rather than the critical connection to the customer. Consequently, the analysts feel their ideas and input are never listened to by management, and they cannot honestly tell the customer a problem will be corrected. So, they begin to question the reason for doing what they are doing.

People who don't feel they're having much effect, beyond putting out fires all day, aren't going to get much satisfaction from their work.

Hard labor. Faced with the high cost of support, some companies try to pressure staff to handle more calls, keep them shorter, and cut down on the less stressful parts of the job such as training and research. Electronic monitoring of workers can be an alienating and destructive tool to push higher quotas. A recent report on electronic monitoring in the workplace by 9 to 5, Working Women Education Fund (Cleveland, Ohio) provides evidence that many companies are using performance monitoring in ways that are destructive to the morale and even health of service workers, as well as to the quality of the service they provide. One case study in the report is about a technical support person who reported that monitoring was used in her company in an effort to drastically increase the number of calls handled, with predictably negative results for staff and customers.

The end result of these stressors can be that much-discussed malady *burnout*. Burnout is defined by Ayala Pines and Elliot

Aronson in their book *Career Burnout: Causes & Cures* (Free Press, 1988) as "a state of physical, emotional, and mental exhaustion caused by long term involvement in situations that are emotionally demanding." When the burnout is bad enough the company loses a tremendous asset, a highly trained support person. As Deborah Fain of Lysis says, "when you lose them it's critical. You lose everything in their minds. It's a killer."

I don't have any easy solutions to the problem of burnout, but here are some suggestions.

Time off the phone. You need to establish a reasonable ratio of online and offline work for the support person. Time off the phones is certainly not wasted, since it adds to the analyst's knowledge as well as longevity. The five hours on/three hours off ratio that Eric Ornas of Borland described is a place to start.

Emphasize training. Putting people on the phones without good training is a little like feeding them to the lions, but in this case even the lions aren't happy.

Provide strong information resources. Back up support people with a strong information infrastructure so they don't have to research the same problems over and over. Beef up product documentation so that users who read it can answer more of their own questions.

Improve the environment. Make the support center pleasant and comfortable. Invest a little more on furniture and equipment.

Build a team. Foster a spirit of cooperation among the support staff so people don't feel isolated. Encourage people to help each other solve problems.

Use monitoring carefully. Managers have lots of new ways to monitor and measure their employees' performance, but they should be used carefully. Big Brother turns everybody off. Focus on qualitative improvement rather than just quantitative. Use monitoring as a training tool.

Create a career path. If you can't give people hope of a better and different job within the organization, you'll lose them, at least the best ones. Putting senior people behind the scenes to deal with the most difficult and interesting problems is one way.

Listen and act on it. Support people know the products and they know a lot about the customers. Make use of this knowledge and give credit for it. Everyone will benefit.

And there's always bribery. On a lighter note, Guy Kawasaki, former software evangelist for Apple, describes another approach to keeping support people happy in a lively chapter on support in his book *The Macintosh Way* (Scott, Foresman and Company, 1990).

> Good support people are also techno-junkies. They want the latest computers, stereos, video players, and automobiles. Companies should buy them as much as they can afford. It can even make good business sense. Customers often associate a company that has the latest tools and toys with leading-edge innovation.

Organizational Issues

To find out where tech support fits within companies, I started with another look at *Soft•Letter*'s tech support survey. They report that software companies charge the costs of support against various budget categories: 30 percent to marketing and sales, 29 percent to general and administration, 15 percent to cost of goods, 12 percent to research and development, and 14 percent to "other."

Companies have tried putting support in various places in their organization charts, according to Eric Ornas of Borland.

> Support has been under marketing, under sales, under product development. Actually, just prior to my arrival I

think it had been under operations at Borland. In the large companies, not in the PC world, but for example in the big iron companies (mainframe manufacturers), they have service as its own division. And I think that's something that we'll be heading towards as these things continue to grow. But I think it makes a lot of sense to be with sales, because of the tie-in to the customer. I've been in a number of different places. I think sales works out quite well.

Deborah Fain of Lysis agrees that marketing is the proper home of support, despite the support's technical aspects.

I think that support is a marketing arm, not a research and development arm, because support is *the* image that the customer has of the product and the company, and that image should not be a technical image. That isn't to say that the answers should not be technical, but the image should not be. As long as support is kept in with research and development and not with marketing, its power and credibility is minimized, whereas if they're aligned with marketing they have a lot more credibility, and a lot more direct feedback into what the product should be. I believe that products should be market driven, not development driven. The correct mission for support, in my mind, is customer service, and certainly the feedback from support should go to research and development, but the mission of support is not to care for R&D.

This view makes sense to me. You support your customers because they've bought your products. You support them because you want them to keep buying and using those products, giving you feedback, and speaking well of your company to other potential customers. These are ultimately marketing concerns.

Selling Support, Inside the Company and Outside

Support's marketing role notwithstanding, its relationships with other parts of the company are crucial. It has vital interests in and contributions to make to research and development and quality assurance, in particular. Naturally, support has to get along with upper management as well.

How does the support center fight for itself, making sure it gets the respect and resources it needs to give good service? What's missing from most support managers, consultant Bill Rose argues, is basic salesmanship—directed at customers, at the company's own sales and research and development staff, and at upper management.

> Most service managers do a pretty good job of servicing their customers, but they do a pretty bad job of letting anybody know what they're doing to service their customers. For example, I've been in organizations that have just installed brand new call management systems, but they've never told anybody that they just spent $45,000 to make them more efficient and to insure that the customers get great service.

Rose is convinced that blowing your support organization's horn is as vital as anything else the support managers do. "It's an absolute necessity that they spend an equal amount of time advertising as they do fixing things and making them operational."

When you're trying to get support's message to your customers, you should avoid the conventional paragraph in marketing literature that talks about your "highly trained support technicians" because nobody's reading that paragraph anymore, Rose says. He recommends getting out the word outside the company with a quality, professionally run advertising campaign. Give customers meaty information about your service levels, staff experience, and new services. Rose suggests you avoid inviting your customers to call unless you *want* a lot of extra calls.

When it comes to selling support within your own company, an important place to start is with the sales staff. Give them the facts about support so they can feature them when making product pitches. Rose says support has traditionally been underplayed in sales presentations—"and oh, by the way, we have great support"—but he sees that changing. To help sales people sell support, Rose offers this advice.

Give them the ammunition. What are you doing right? We're resolving this many calls. This is how many people we have. Those kinds of things—bundling and packaging that will enhance the image of support throughout the organization, whether it be through an internal newsletter or memos presentations to the sales people.

Support's relationship with research and development is central, since we generally depend on them to solve the problems we can't solve internally. Research and development, according to Rose, always wants to know "How many calls are you passing me? Are you efficient in what you do?" He finds that development often has a inaccurate picture of just how well support is screening them from unnecessary work.

It never ceases to amaze me how surprised they are when you tell them that 85 percent of the issues are actually being resolved in the support center and only 15 percent come their way, because they feel they're getting 100 percent. So one of the things we want to do is to put strong service levels in place and publicize them to the developers.

Rose suggests going to development's staff meetings and informally discussing your service levels, your proposed changes, and your plans for the future.

Dealing with upper management is another story. Rose says that when support management goes in to upper management to ask for another $35,000 worth of support furniture, it's typically seen as "just dollar signs" with no clear benefit to the company. To counter that attitude, here's what Rose suggests.

What support managers need to do in that position is to make sure that they have cost-justified every expenditure and be able to put in dollars and cents either what kind of savings or increased revenue they project. What is the value of the services that we currently deliver, and why do we need to spend a little bit of money on it?

Answering those questions for upper management will put you in a lot better position to win the support game.

Service Sells

After years in the background, support is moving toward center stage. Some companies are building pre-eminent positions by offering superior support and making sure everyone knows it. Manufacturers are beginning to proclaim their product support policies on packaging and in full-page ads, instead of hiding their hotline numbers from users. The debate still continues about whether support should be fee-based or included in the price of the product, but both sides are putting major resources in place to deliver quality service. People are beginning to make successful careers in the technical support centers, and the increasing professionalism is having an effect on customer satisfaction. Progress isn't universal and customers are still not satisfied with the support they're getting with all of their computer tools, but when support is strengthened, both users and the computer industry itself are bound to benefit.

Internal Support

For millions of people, going to work means booting up a PC. In a few short years one-person offices and globe-spanning corporations have come to depend on microcomputers for their fundamental operations. Now they're learning how to help their employees when computer trouble strikes, because the cost of computer downtime and lost worker productivity can be staggering.

Though microcomputers are often referred to as "personal," most organizations have learned that when the technology starts to give its user trouble, the ramifications are anything but personal. The user's individual productivity suffers immediately as he struggles to find a solution, but the damage can quickly spread to the work group, department, or even the whole organization. In this chapter we'll focus on ways organizations have found to help their employees deal with computer problems as quickly and painlessly as possible.

The Help Function—Past, Present, and Future

Larger companies had gradually mastered most of the problems involved with centralized mainframe and moderately distributed minicomputer management when PCs came along with their capacity to make each desktop a source of computer power and headaches. In larger organizations, micro technology hasn't displaced the mainframes and minis that businesses have depended on for decades, though that "downsizing" process is picking up steam. Micro technology has created a powerful, diffuse presence, though, that traditional mainframe management styles have a hard time accommodating. Classic data processing management stressed centralized control every step of the way. Computers cost a fortune, were hard to use, and had to be controlled by experts. A company's data was its lifeblood, and the data's integrity had to be staunchly protected.

The MIS (Management Information Services) organizations that lived in the glass houses and ran the mainframes were hardly eager to embrace the upstart micros that started showing up in the early '80s. Compared to mainframes and minis, PCs are instruments of anarchy. In some places MIS continues to be responsible for managing PCs. In many other places a separate, sometimes subordinate organization called an Information Center (IC) was developed for this purpose, often reporting to MIS. We'll consider the task this department faces in "Managing Microcomputers" below.

Wherever big companies have decided to put the management of PC technology within their organization charts, they've generally found they need to establish a group within the company devoted to helping computer users with their problems. Often called the help desk or support center (I'll use both terms), this group might have started back in the old days helping users on terminals who had trouble accessing the mainframe. Now the help desk has its hands full trying to keep PC users happy, or at least productive. In many organizations there are several help desks, one still devoted to mainframe access, one for PCs, and perhaps one for network issues and telecommunications. Throw in other phone numbers for hardware installation, maintenance, and telecommunications issues, and users are often confused when they have to decide who to call. Even support staff themselves may have trouble figuring out who's supposed to handle what. In addition, getting past territorial imperatives and politics may often be tough. There seems to be a trend now toward increased consolidation of MIS and IC functions, fueled no doubt by the fact that more and more mainframe functions are being taken over by networked PCs.

From the users' point of view, this consolidation could be a great thing. Eventually a single help desk for all technology questions will probably have to emerge if users are to be helped quickly and efficiently. If this one support center is not able to provide immediate solutions to all classes of problems (hardware, software, etc.), it should at least be able to forward problems to the appropriate specialist without forcing the user to keep dialing for help.

Managing Micro-computers

"End-user computing" is a term that's often used to describe computing on micros and other platforms where users have hands-on control of basic operations. Managing this ever-growing mass of technology is a challenging, sometimes almost overwhelming new career. Here's a partial list of the tasks involved in managing end-user computing.

- Determine organization's and users' needs.

- Assess and select hardware and software.

- Justify costs to upper management.

- Hire, train, and supervise technical and clerical staff.

- Negotiate with vendors and handle purchases.

- Install, inventory, and maintain hardware.

- Install and upgrade software.

- Maintain computer security.

- Develop specialized applications.

- Train and consult with users.

- Help users when they have problems and questions.

It's that last function that's the main subject of this chapter, but many of the others have important implications for user support. I'll comment on six that require significant input from the support center.

PROJECT PLAN

- Assessing users' needs accurately requires clear understanding of what kinds of problems they've had in the past, what kind of help they've asked for, and what they've said about their needs. All of this information comes through the help desk.

- Choosing the best hardware and software should entail careful attention to the support policies of the manufacturer as well as how difficult the products are to use and support. Keeping control of the number of different products being used is vital if those products are to be supported properly.

- Convincing management of the cost-effectiveness of new technology requires intimate understanding of users' problems and needs. The support center's documentation of users' problems can back up purchasing arguments.

- Maintaining computer security requires help desk vigilance. Support staff may be in a position to quickly spot infection by viruses and to help enforce the organization's policies on un-authorized (possibly pirated) software.

- Support staff may be involved with application development projects, and will certainly be called on to provide user assistance once the applications are in place.

- Support staff are in an excellent position to judge users' training needs and in many organizations may be the best ones to actually carry out training.

Given these interconnections, it's clear that user assistance—the technical support or help desk function—should be seen as part of the whole of microcomputer management, rather than as a completely self-contained activity. In small organizations you can see this integration in action. A few PC professionals (or a busy individual) may wear many hats, taking hotline calls, giving training, choosing, installing and troubleshooting hardware and software. In mid-sized organizations, there's often a separate help desk unit, but its staff may have many microcomputer management roles to play in addition to answering the hotline. I'll try to link user assistance issues with other aspects of microcomputer management whenever possible.

The Help Desk Mission: Productivity

Just what is the mission of the help desk or support center in an organization? In keeping with contemporary business practice, it's common for PC support departments to feel the need to have a "mission statement," a simple declaration of what they do in the context of the overall company goals. An example might be "To help MegaCorp's employees use computer technology productively to make and sell our products." Whether such a statement is given lip service or taken as a sacred trust depends on the culture of the organization and individual attitudes, but such guidelines are too simple to give much guidance to support staff in making hard decisions about what they should do to help users.

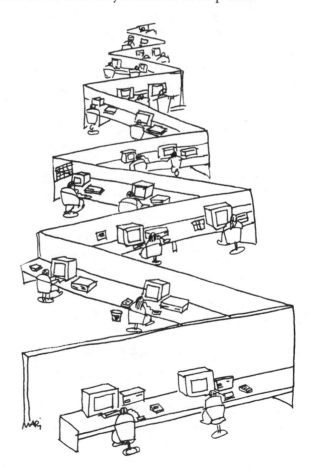

I sought some ideas from an experienced observer of the field, Elliot Masie of the Association for Training and Support. Masie has been involved in support and training for many years and regularly gives seminars on these subjects. When I asked Masie about the mission of support, he said, "In internal support, if you allow yourself to be all that you can be, your job is to help other people be productive. That productivity will come from doing troubleshooting, training, developing help sheets for them, fixing their machine, whatever it takes." Contrasting internal support with that given by manufacturers and dealers, Masie adds, "You're not limited to just the system. Many of the blocks to productivity are not system failures, but the work flow that gets created around the system." That internal support people have more responsibility to deal with the entire work process can also become a nightmare in Masie's view. The support person "may be a techie who is now being told, 'Hold it, my figures didn't come out right on this mortgage!' and the techie may not know mortgages at all. So there's always a risk that you may not be able to help them, or you may get in over your head."

Masie is right. The job of support is to help people be more productive, and an exclusive focus on the technology may make it impossible to see the best way to achieve that. Maybe the user shouldn't be using a computer at all but a pencil and paper to solve a particular problem, or maybe the user is looking at the wrong problem. Yet the reality of most organizations, at least larger ones, is that support staff only have contact with users who need, or think they need, specific computer solutions. And the support staff's training and experience is focused on the use of specific software and hardware tools.

In the long run, real productivity improvements probably will require support people who have both computer and business expertise. Many organizations seem to be beginning to foster this cross-training by sending their help desk and other computer people out into the organization for study visits to see how the technology is really being used.

Another way to get support people more deeply involved in finding productivity solutions for users instead of simply waiting for them to call with problems is suggested by *PC Week* columnist and corporate technology manager Cheryl Currid. She advocates a new kind of technology support person she calls a "software evangelist." I asked her to contrast this position with the more traditional support roles.

> The software evangelist differs from a traditional help-desk person or trainer in some subtle but important ways. Evangelists are mission oriented while help-desk and trainer folks are mechanics oriented. Here's what I mean.
>
> Usually help-desk people don't leave their desks. They answer "how" questions over the phone. Generally the questions are mechanical in nature, such as, "How do you use the @SUM command in Lotus?" "How do you set the print area for an Excel spreadsheet?" "How do you set up tables in WordPerfect 5.1?"
>
> Similarly, trainers deal in the mechanics of software. They follow the course outline, showing users how to do certain things. Trainers might expand out a little, showing users little known tricks or traps.
>
> Evangelists differ because they are mission focused. They are using technology to solve whole problems. An evangelist steps into the process early and helps the user determine which tools to use. Then the evangelists follows the work process, making sure the user is doing things right.

Achieving Organizational Productivity with Multi-level Support

The purpose of the support function is to foster productivity of the organization's employees or members, and while this usually focuses attention on the productivity of the end-users, there's another group whose productivity is important. Internal support operations serve to protect the time of the information center staff itself by preventing end-user questions and problems from constantly interrupting technical projects and soaking up the time of the most highly-trained and paid personnel. If there is no help desk to field questions, users will have to button-hole programmers or other technical staff to get help, with predictable consequences for information center productivity.

One model that's prevalent in large organizations today sees the help desk as the first line of support, staffed by generalists who attempt to answer as high a percentage as possible of questions.

When the help desk staff is stumped they escalate problems to more specialized technicians. Dave Kuches is a consultant who leads seminars on designing support operations under the auspices of the Help Desk Institute. He learned the model during his years at IBM, and though it originated in the mainframe world it applies on smaller platforms as well. Kuches describes it this way.

> There have been studies that said the help desk should be able to resolve a high percentage of those problems coming in. The help desk people are not necessarily highly paid, so you have hopefully some return on investment if you can get the help desk to resolve 80 percent of the problems coming in, relying on written procedures. You find out that a lot of the problems out there are procedural problems, so you get that knock-off rate. If they're hitting 80 percent resolution, that leaves 20 percent.
>
> We define it according to levels. The help desk would be Level One. Level Two typically is your operations function, system operations, network operations. They get their turn and get the 20 percent that the help desk didn't resolve. Maybe they're a little better paid than the help desk, but now we're buffering them, and they're getting problems that they can work on and they're not being bothered by trivial problems. We found those numbers to be 15 percent. So the operational level of the organization is able to knock off 15 percent and the 5 percent goes on to Level Three, which I define as technical support. These are people that are very specialized in the various products in the various systems, and typically they're the higher paid resources in the organization.

Some people use a slightly different model. They might call the first ones to answer the phone "entry level" support and limit their purview to the most basic technical issues. These folks escalate most calls to an appropriate Level One support person, someone with significant expertise in the area where the problem is focused. The most highly trained experts would then constitute a Level Two. If the help desk is handling calls on multiple platforms and technologies—mainframe, LAN, telecommunications, for example—your first line support people might not be able to achieve Kuches's 80 percent resolution rate, but however you break it down, a multi-level system is a sensible way to do business if you're large enough to maintain it. Many companies are simply too small to employ several levels of support staff. Yet among those who have the resources to adopt effective multi-level support it's far from universal, according to Dave Kuches.

There are some alternative ways of insulating information center staff from "trivial" user problems besides the classic multi-level support model suggested by Kuches. In some organizations, the information center staff put in a limited, scheduled amount of time on the help desk, working on other projects between their stints on the phone. Some organizations staff the help desk with people whose training is more clerical than technical. They function more as dispatchers than problem-solvers, taking problem descriptions and forwarding them to specialists who may call or visit the user. The problem with this arrangement is that although highly trained technicians are insulated from the initial user call, they will have to talk to most users eventually because the help desk itself isn't solving any of the problems. The user has no chance of getting immediate help from someone with technical knowledge. Hours can go by before effective help is delivered.

To get the full benefit of multi-level support, management has to create a team of help desk staffers with enough technical knowledge to solve a high percentage of problems and to effectively escalate the rest.

Colleagues or Customers?

Another question arises. If internal support exists to increase the productivity of the organization's employees who use computers, how should those users be thought of? A strong argument is made nowadays in computing circles that the users should really be seen as *customers*, and that they should be treated with the respect and deference that businesses ideally lavish on their customers. As William E. Perry wrote in *Government Computer News*, "If you have customers, you must serve them. You don't have to serve end-users." If you have customers, you have to take their complaints seriously, strive to be responsive to their needs, listen carefully to them, and try to please them. You have to engage in that very difficult process called customer service. Perry advocates setting up a central customer service department in MIS just as in a department store, designed to field comments, requests, and complaints. It's not a bad idea. The help desk as presently constituted is there to answer questions and solve problems, but it's rarely empowered to go much further.

There are counterarguments to the "users as customers" position. Some managers say that the organization's real customers are the people on the outside who buy its products and services, and that every internal unit should stay focused on that customer relationship. Another argument is that focusing on customer satisfaction can sometimes keep you from doing what you need to do. Elliot Masie agrees.

> I may need to do some things to provide effective computer support that piss off the people that I'm providing it to, but may yield productivity. I may say, "No, go get your manual—I'm not going to give you any support without your manual!" Now I'm certainly not going to get any customer satisfaction for it, but I am leveraging the corporate investment in that manual and that user and that system by doing that.

Putting aside the question of whether it might sometimes be more economical for the user to call for help instead of grappling with the manual for a half hour, Masie has a good point. Support has some "policing" functions to carry out that make it hard for support staff to think of themselves as purely a customer service operation. The problem is that there is more than one customer! Support is supposed to serve the people who own the company as much as the employees. Maybe more, if you were to talk to those owners. The folks that sign the checks have priorities that are not always identical with those of their employees. Responsibilities like watching out for pirated software, enforcing sound data security practices, and getting folks to read manuals are likely to fall on support's shoulders, like it or not, and they may not always make support popular with users. Denying that there are sometimes conflicts in these responsibilities isn't going to make things easier.

Maybe we need a new way to think about the relationship of help desk to user. Start with a customer service orientation, add some collegial equality and cooperation ("We're all working together for the greater good"), and throw in a little of the authority of the doctor or teacher, the kind that makes it possible to occasionally administer unpalatable medicine or homework assignments. Not every answer or prescription will make the user immediately happy, but if the help desk staff do their job right, there will be enough confidence in their authority and service orientation to make users keep the faith.

Supporting PCs is tough and the challenges come from all sides—users, upper management, technology, staff—all exerting pressure, all demanding their due. Let's look at some of the big issues facing internal support and some of the solutions that are emerging.

Challenge: Shrinking Resources

Despite the increasing dependence of most businesses on micros, corporations seem to be reducing their investment in support. *PC Week*'s 1988 survey of its 500-plus member Corporate Advisory Panel found that each support employee was supporting 77.5 PCs, up from 73.4 the year before. That was the second straight year that the survey found a worsening of the ratio of support staff to users. Although more recent data isn't available, there's no reason to think the trend has reversed. Glance at the information center press or listen to micro managers and the trend is clear. The belt-tightening going on in American companies has squeezed support operations harder than most. There's tremendous pressure to keep head count low, despite increasing demand.

Overall, corporations don't seem to be meeting the challenge of microcomputer support, according to most of the indicators. Cheryl Currid of *PC Week* says, "I'd give corporate America a 'C-minus' grade. In other words, many companies are doing a barely adequate job. Of course, every company is a little different and some companies are moving forward with programs that make computer literacy a part of the scene. My best guess is that in the short term, corporate results are spotty."

Currid says many corporate leaders don't understand the need for support. "I believe there is a feeling that users are smart now and don't need any help." These upper-level managers are wrong, she thinks, adding, "There's a lot of work to be done before companies should stop investing in end-user support. Anyone who thinks that 'Joe Average Corporate User' is ready to fly solo with microcomputer technology hasn't looked inside a few Lotus spreadsheets lately." Currid thinks users are headed in the right direction. "Time is maturing the group. Users are smarter than they were a few years ago, but they aren't ready to go it alone. A combination of time and tools will make things better in the next few years."

Currid thinks that another reason for reduced resources is that the benefits of microcomputers may have been oversold. She says, "There is a feeling that benefits from microcomputers are limited at best and already maxed out. There could be a feeling of disappointment. Microcomputers were supposed to be the great boost to productivity. In many places, however, that is simply not the case."

Elliot Masie of the Association for Training and Support describes support's funding struggle.

Support becomes an elastic function. It tends never to be funded or established arithmetically. Nobody says, "I have a thousand users, I need x number of people doing user support." Rather, it's elastic. You start with one support person who gets swamped so you add another one, and you build the body count until it gets too big. Then you have a reduction in force, and you start all over again next year.

Why this lack of a solid foundation? Masie sees support trapped between two negative forces.

Support is trapped on one side by the publishers and developers of software, who continue to promulgate the mythology that their stuff is easy to use. And as long as I've just paid a million dollars, let's say, for a hospital patient information system that's easy to use, why do I need to have six people in a help desk, or an information center, or whatever we want to call it?

Support is trapped on the other side by the fact that many users essentially don't want to internalize their system, so their investment in gaining competence is often minimal. As opposed to learning the system, they learn the most minimal slice of the system, and then when their work changes or their requirements change, they come up against a brick wall of their own ignorance. Now I don't blame the user. I often blame the manager of the user.

Proving What It's Worth

How do you prove that support is vital to the organization's productivity, that it deserves better than it's getting? Though the folks who take calls from the users know they're providing an important service, that they're overworked, and perhaps not able to do as much for users as they should because of tight budgets, upper management can be mighty skeptical of any expense that doesn't contribute directly to the bottom line. Since management is fond of measuring everything, I sought out ideas on how to measure the costs and benefits of support. Dave Kuches has studied the subject.

Of course, the costs are easily determined—people's salaries, the space they're taking up, the equipment they're using. But looking at the other side, the quantifiable benefits are more difficult to measure. I usually start with the cost for the people and factor in how much you improve their productivity (or *lose* productivity). What do those numbers translate into? It's very difficult. You've got to appeal to intuition. "It's good to do because it's good to do!"

What you *can* do is compare salary rates with and without an efficient help desk in place. Say, "We're going to put in a help desk function and beef it up. That will have a direct impact on our technical specialists, our (high-level) technical support people, because they'll only get the problems that we need their level of expertise on." So you take their salary rates, and you may have to guess that you're going to improve their productivity rate by one percent, two percent. Then you can start getting some tangible numbers.

When it comes to outages—trying to translate that number—if you've got X people on a LAN and they're doing data entry for a payroll application, and they're down for an hour, you can work off their salary rates and try to translate that back into quantifiable numbers. But mostly you end up saying, "It's intuitively obvious. We're going to improve the overall productivity of the organization."

I suggested to Kuches at this point that a useful strategy might be to play off the general feelings in the organization about things not being as good as they should be. He agreed.

Right. You start dealing with noise levels. If you're getting complaints from the user community, that's an indicator that something's not right. And a lot of times those complaints are not necessarily with problems, they're about getting support with problems. If those problems are not getting resolved, then Data Processing's the bad guy and Data Processing doesn't like to be the bad guy, so let's take care of it. So you can deal with it from that whole perspective.

It comes down to the whole concept of service, delivery of service. There's an organization that's managing technology. Hopefully that technology is there to assist the rest of the business in doing a better job, and the users of that technology become customers or clients. You want them to have a good perspective, a good attitude that the organization is responsible for that technology. This is where the help desk plays a public relations role, because the help desk can have a direct impact on how the user thinks and feels about the technology and the managers of the technology. We're constantly, often unconsciously, measuring. "They did a good job." "They gave me good service." "They didn't give me good service." That applies to the technology.

We're back to intangibles: good service, public relations, productivity, and positive attitudes toward the people who are managing the technology. Numbers don't tell the real story of what support is contributing, because it's nearly impossible to measure the time you've saved the users or the added power you've given them. Nonetheless, as support consultant Bill Rose said in Chapter 1, *Manufacturer Support,* you have to count the beans. Count the number of PCs in the organization that you're supporting (many managers don't have a clue). Count the number of calls the help desk has handled this month and compare it to last year. Count the calls by department of the caller, product they're calling about, and type of issue. Count your average time on the phone and compare it to what it was last month and last year. Be vigilant for any numbers that show concrete gains in user productivity because of support's efforts, or in support's productivity because of improvements it's made.

There are other kinds of evidence that show you've had an impact besides statistics. Collect your thank you notes from satisfied users and write down positive comments made about your work. Present them along with the cold numbers when it's time to fight for a bigger budget.

KNOWLEDGE BASE

Tools to Keep Track

CALLER INFO
CALL DURATION
TIME/DATE
NATURE OF PROB
RESOLUTION
PRODUCT LINE
STATUS CODE
P - PENDING
C = CLOSED
T = TXFER

SECOND LEVEL

MEMO FIELD

Fundamental to keeping the kinds of statistics just mentioned, as well as tracking individual user problems and comments is a well-designed call-tracking system. Each and every call or other transaction handled by the help desk, no matter how "trivial," must be accurately logged. Elsewhere in this book I describe various call-tracking software products and information techniques, but the essential point here is that every call, every question and answer, must be documented. I've mentioned the importance of statistics in justifying the costs of the support operation to upper management, but there are other purposes that are just as important. The data that's collected—questions and answers, products covered, call lengths, identities of callers and their departments—might seem like just that much more "information overload" for management, but if it's properly analyzed and evaluated, it can become valuable. For example, it can point out the following things.

- Products that are getting used most or causing most problems

- Individuals or departments that are in need of more training or supplemental documentation

- Problem trends—issues that are emerging as significant user productivity killers

- Specific problems that recur in different places and different guises

- Trends in help desk productivity

Since one of the biggest challenges of support work is its reactive, fire-fighting, crisis-oriented nature, any well-planned initiative that prevents or reduces problems is like gold. Having solid information makes it possible for the help desk or the information center as a whole to take a more proactive stance with regard to helping users and managing technology. If certain products cause undue problems, maybe they should be replaced. If data shows users need more training, why not recommend it instead of waiting for user demand? If odd problems are recurring, try doing a little research on the causes. All of these steps take resources, but if you have data you can estimate some concrete long-term savings that will be achieved.

Analysis of the data is the key. It's no simple trick to do, and there's no magic software to do it for you, though some standard database reports can help. Analysis means taking the time to read all the call records and note what they indicate. It means deriving categories that are meaningful in the context of your particular organization and counting which calls fall into which categories. It means calling on the judgment of the people on the phones to report their impressions and hunches about patterns they've perceived in their calls, and allowing them the freedom from time pressure needed to make careful notes on each call. Often the people on the phones are the best ones to do at least the preliminary analysis of call records, and this can be a very productive offline task when they're not taking calls. Analysis has to be done regularly and methodically. The results should be made available to interested parties—to management, to the people on the phones, and, selectively, to users themselves, perhaps as part of a computer user's newsletter.

Challenge: Increasing Technical Demands

A few short years ago microcomputer technology was pretty simple, even if it didn't seem that way at the time. PC XTs, ATs, a handful of applications, an occasional LAN installation to make it interesting. Things have changed. No one can deny that the technology is getting more and more complex, the technical issues tougher. Should you stick with the traditional software that most users are familiar with, or try some of the cheaper, more feature-rich competitive products? Should the company migrate to OS/2, Windows? Now or when? What to do about hundreds of completely functional but virtually obsolete 286s and 8088s? What about those pesky Macs that keep getting smuggled in? Should all mainframe applications be downsized to networked PCs? What network? What about the integrity of vital company data?

The corollary to increasing technical complexity is tougher support challenges. There are simply more hardware and software products out there, more diversity in the kinds of projects being undertaken, and more opportunities for problematic interactions. Help desks have their hands full trying to keep up.

Controlling the Flood

One of the most important responses to burgeoning technology is the struggle to control the introduction of new products. From support's point of view, everything is much simpler when there are a limited number of standard products used throughout the organization. A limited number of standard products means support staff needs less training and can develop deeper knowledge of each product. Consultant Allen Taylor from Computer Power in Midway City, California, says the benefits of standardization extend beyond help staff to users themselves.

If you have one standard kind of personal computer that you always get, and you always configure it the same with the same amount of memory and the same disk drive, and you always put on the same standard packages—one standard word processor, one standard spreadsheet, one standard graphics package—so that all the people in your organization are using the same standard software, that will make your support effort that much easier.

It will also make it easier for users, because in any real organization, people are going to be transferring from one department to another on a continual basis. If somebody has been using WordPerfect for the last three years in accounting and now they get transferred over to engineering and they're using WordStar over there, there's a whole learning curve to go through. Why go through the grief? Why not have everybody use the same thing? Now unfortunately you're going to run into some flack from your users, because people have their own software that they're comfortable with, that they're happy with. But in the long run, you're better off if you can establish a standard and make it stick—standard hardware and standard software.

Of course, you'll have to constantly be doing evaluation to make sure that you do have the best software that's available and it's meeting your users' needs, and if you find as time goes on that your software is no longer meeting your users needs, you have to be willing to make that shift to something new that meets those needs better, and in that case you want to convert everybody over all at the same time.

Taylor is obviously talking about an ideal situation, attainable in organizations where PC management is strongly centralized and where it always has been. Many managers find that kind of complete control is unattainable, that business units demand and get the products they want to do their work. In such situations a tactic that helps keep support demands within reason is to maintain different levels of support for different products. By spelling out the level of support available for each product, the information center at least makes users aware that there are benefits to sticking with the standard products and extra costs involved in deviating from the list. The drawback is that if departments go ahead with maverick products, they will have to find their own support sources and thus will undermine the help desk's position as the central source of support in the organization.

A list. These products are completely supported. Support staff are fully trained on these products, all technical literature is kept up to date, and installation and upgrades are usually carried out by the IC.

B list. Less support is guaranteed for these products. Hotline help may not be available or fewer staff are trained. Technical literature may not be maintained. Product upgrades must be carried out by the users.

C list. This list contains every product not contained on the A or B lists. Business units may purchase these products but there is no support available from the information center or the help desk. Some managers soften this a little. "We don't refuse to help them, but we don't promise that our answers are correct."

Getting Help from the Horse's Mouth

One of the results of the increasing complexity of the technology is that the problems themselves are more difficult, requiring deeper knowledge of the products themselves and their interactions with other products. The help desk, which is generally staffed by technically astute people proud of their own problem-solving abilities, may make things harder for itself by trying to figure out all the answers instead of simply calling manufacturers and asking for help with tough problems. Managers have to encourage support staff to "give up" when appropriate and call those hotlines. They must also use their leverage with manufacturers to improve tech support services. Corporate buyers will often subscribe to manufacturers' premium fee-based support services, and they must make a point of monitoring how well those services are delivering.

Challenge: Different Types of Users

As we've seen, economic pressures mean that support centers are dealing with more users, more calls, with less staff. The users themselves may be becoming more diverse and therefore more difficult to support. New workers may not be well-equipped to handle computers due to limited exposure and poor education. Temporary workers, relied on more and more, may have had little or no training in the right products. Mergers, acquisitions, and reorganizations may suddenly bring on board a whole new raft of users accustomed to other tools and procedures. Everyone from the greenest beginner to the most advanced PC expert can call for help and the support staff has to be flexible enough to deal with each special need.

One way to distinguish users is according to their willingness to deal with change in the tools and methods they use in their work. Sociologists who study the way new technology and ideas spread throughout a society have distinguished five types of people.

Experimenters. These folks love new technology, always want the latest, and love to push it to its limits.

Early adopters. Not quite as avid as the Experimenters, they are nonetheless eager to put technology to practical use.

Pragmatists. This group constitutes the majority of the user population. They'll use the new technology when it's proven and they're sure it's here to stay.

Late adopters. Hesitant to get involved in computer technology, they'll accept it when they're forced to.

Resisters. These people hate the very idea of learning to use computers and actively reject the intrusion of high technology into their lives.

Target Your Audience

Clearly, the first people to join the PC revolution came from the top of the list and as it marches on, the ranks of users are drawn from people further down. Those two first categories represent the power users and PC gurus. They put pressure on the organization to get the newest and best machines and software. They won't bother you with simple support problems—they'd be ashamed— but they might just take pleasure in bringing you a real stumper now and then. A number of micro managers have reported success in keeping these folks productively busy by giving them plenty of new hardware and software to evaluate. Seriously, the information center has a lot to learn from power users, who often know more about the technology than its own staff. Later on we'll talk about ways to enlist their talents in the support of users.

The pragmatists represent the majority of users, and, of course, the majority of callers. These folks neither love nor hate computers, but they'll use them to do their jobs. They're unlikely to get excited about learning new tricks, unless there's an immediate practical payoff. Support staff might have the most success with these people by emphasizing that the computer is simply a tool to do a job and focusing on that job rather than the technology itself. Knowing more about the kinds of projects your users are doing with their computers is probably going to help you serve the pragmatists. Bear in mind that new users are likely to be of the pragmatic persuasion. If they were born techies they'd probably not be beginners anymore. Keep explanations to them focused on solving practical problems unless they express an interest in going deeper.

The last two categories, the "late adopters" and the "resisters," can be tough to help, although true resisters may never get close enough to a computer to have any problems. Understandably enough, a certain percentage of the population just doesn't like computers, but the march of history is forcing more of them to use the infernal gadgets, like it or not. Nothing the support center can do is guaranteed to make these people into computerphiles— though stranger things have happened—but a little patience, encouragement, and good humor from the support staff may help make them friends.

One of the most valuable things a help desk can do for both novices and computerphobic types is to gradually guide them toward self-sufficiency. The primary tool of self-sufficiency, of course, is user documentation, and though nobody seems to like reading it much, it can help if the help desk has a policy of asking all callers to follow along in the manual if the solution is to be found there. It's counterproductive, though, to pretend to less-sophisticated users that manuals have all the answers or that they're all well-written and easy to use. It's much better to commiserate with callers about how murky and abstruse the documentation is at the same time you demonstrate that it is useful and can be deciphered.

Support and Training

Every organization seems to handle training differently, but the help desk should have a role to play in guiding users to training opportunities the company provides. I asked Elliot Masie how businesses are coordinating support and training functions.

> They're usually not coordinated well. It would make absolute sense for them to be. In fact, there are three functions—training, support and documentation. We call it the TSD model. Those three functions all share the same bottom line mission in the organization, in that they're all involved in user productivity.
>
> Sometimes they're coordinated; sometimes they're uncoordinated. Sometimes one of them is outsourced. For example, the training may be done by an external vendor, and the support may be done by an external vendor. It would make lots of sense—and we've been advocating this organizationally—to have training, support, and documentation be single sourced, where they all are at least coordinated, if not centrally managed. But because of the nature of training—it's a very political area—it could end up being controlled by any number of players.

At the very least, help desk staff need to know what the company's training program is and be encouraged to advertise training opportunities to users who might benefit. They should have some valuable insights into the training needs of the users and be able to evaluate whether training is having the desired effect. Support staff may be the most logical candidates for inhouse trainers, though they need some training in training techniques before they're put in front of a class.

Training the Managers

Some information centers have found that one of the best ways to help users is to have a talk with their managers now and then. In many cases, managers are not in the front line of corporate microcomputing, and don't have much knowledge of what their staff is doing with the technology. They may not know about the importance of such basics as training, regular backups, documentation, and computer security. Talking to managers about their responsibility for maintaining "computer discipline" in their departments goes a long way to preventing disasters and reducing demand for help desk services.

Challenge: Staff Burnout

Like their colleagues who do support in other contexts, help desk and other internal support staff are often subject to stress and burnout, which can be defined as a drastic decline in enthusiasm for one's job. Several reasons for the stress are commonly cited.

- Lack of control over work flow

- Constantly dealing with problems and people who are upset

- Repetitive, tedious questions

- Insufficient training and backup support

- Lack of professional rewards, recognition, and career path

Observers have noted a tendency for burnout to show up among hotline staff after 18 months to two years, which is, ironically, about the time their training and experience *should* be bringing them to full productivity. Obviously, managers have an interest in reducing stress and at least delaying burnout as long as possible.

In the previous chapter, manufacturer support managers discussed several ways to reduce stress, and those ideas are just as applicable to internal support. Setting a reasonable limit to time spent on the hotline and other intensive public interaction is the first rule. Its corollary is to find productive and enjoyable projects for staff to pursue when offline. Training, both inhouse and offsite, developing applications, analyzing problem data, and evaluating products are all valuable activities that most support people would probably enjoy as a complement to answering the hotline.

Another key to happier, longer-lasting staff is a viable, believable career path within the organization—a sense of optimism about one's future if one stays. Without it, looking for greener pastures is only natural.

The Right Staff

One of the first places to start in preventing burnout is in the selection of your staff. Not everyone has the personality or skills to thrive and succeed in a help desk or other support role. Consultant Allen Taylor says you're not likely to find the perfect individual, but you can look for fundamentals and train for the rest.

The help desk requires a combination of technical expertise, communication skills, and personality traits that is not often found in a single individual. Ideal help desk people are rare. If you can't find the ideal person—and chances are that you can't—hire the person with the right personality traits. He or she can learn the technical information on the job. It is much more difficult to teach a technically qualified person to change their personality than it is to teach a person who has the right personality the technical details.

Taylor lists a number of personality traits to look for. "The number one, two, and three desired traits are patience." Callers are often upset, even abusive and it takes patience and an even temper to deal with their problems.

Another quality to look for Taylor calls "relative contentment." You don't want someone who's looking to quickly move up and out, because it takes a long time to bring a support person to full productivity. And you want them to be content with their pay, which is not likely to be the highest in the MIS hierarchy.

Of course, you want someone who gets enjoyment from solving problems, but also someone who likes to teach. A support person is going to spend a lot of time explaining solutions to people. Many technically astute people love to tackle tough problems, but just don't like explaining anything, especially to novices.

Look for someone who thrives on demanding work, Taylor says. Keep in mind that a support job isn't for people who like to kick back and watch the clock.

In addition to these personality traits, Taylor points out some mental skills that are important.

A person should be a good communicator, on the phone, in person, and in writing. Support work may involve much more than just telephone contact. Writing clearly is important for documenting calls as well as creating reports, and there are often times when support people will need to communicate with management or users face to face.

Look for someone who is a good analytical thinker. One component of that ability is asking good questions. A big part of troubleshooting is figuring out what you need to know and asking the user to supply it.

Taylor suggests looking for people who can juggle a couple of seemingly contradictory needs. They must be able to focus strongly on one problem and to keep track of several tasks at one time. When support people are on the hotline, they must keep attention tightly on the matter at hand. Yet they must also be able to keep several background tasks from falling through the cracks.

Finally, according to Taylor, good support people have to be generalists. They need to be at least conversant with all the hardware, software, and procedures the users will be calling about. Their knowledge of all products may not be extremely deep, but it needs to be broad enough that they can understand the context of the users' calls and know where to look for a solution.

New Ideas

If the model of internal support provided by an inhouse staff operating out of MIS or IC is still predominant, it's not without some competition. As we've seen, belt-tightening and a tighter focus on the bottom line have eroded the resources for full-blown internal help desk functions and many companies have been looking for alternatives. We'll look at a couple here.

Peer Support

It's only natural. When people have problems with their computers they're just as likely to ask the person at the next desk as the help desk, especially if that colleague is a capable computer user. The only problem is that the knowledgeable colleague may get overloaded by requests for help, and find his own productivity suffering as a result. And what acknowledgement does he get for his time spent helping colleagues?

Some companies have begun to mine this vein of inhouse expertise to augment beleaguered PC support staffs. They've sought ways to formalize and control a process that's been going on since microcomputers first came on the scene—users helping users. Sometimes one computer guru is called something like "Departmental Computing Coordinator," and given responsibility for acting as first-line support to all his departmental colleagues.

A more elaborate version of this approach is being developed at Corning Corporation in Corning, New York. Back in 1988, Corning found itself, like many other companies, facing increasing demand for support services, a fixed head count, increasingly complex technical demands, and less than universal praise from users for its service levels. Carol Hartwig, then the head of client support services, the user assistance part of the IS department, knew that though her department was overloaded with help calls, the calls weren't evenly distributed. Some departments almost never called. She and consultant Barbara Braverman of Computer

Thinking in Rochester, New York set out to investigate how users in one 120-member business unit were currently handling their computer problems and getting training. They mailed out questionnaires and did some in-depth interviewing.

What they found was that most users in the department preferred dealing with someone they worked with rather than the company help desk. Much of the training users had received was also from peers, and they rated it higher than formal training. The problems with this informal, user-to-user support were fairly predictable.

- Users delivered support to some of their colleagues but not to others.

- Users were willing to give support only when their workload allowed.

- Users weren't willing to take on more responsibility without formal recognition.

- It wasn't clear to users how to get help from IS if peer support was insufficient.

Encouraged that the elements were present to put together a new support strategy, Hartwig and Braverman created a four-person team of IS representatives, department members, and a consultant to come up with a workable design. They developed a plan for a "user resource network" that included three different departmental support roles.

- Proficient user. The "power user" or "guru" that we all know about is someone who is competent in one or more technologies and is willing to help other users.

- Mentor. A mentor is a proficient user who helps novice users increase their computer skills. Not all proficient users are mentors.

- Facilitator. This is a manager or supervisor who promotes the development of proficient users and mentors and takes management responsibility for technology in the department. Each business unit will probably have one facilitator.

The idea was to build the first user resource network in the unit that was originally studied, see how it worked, and then gradually spread the concept to other units. Implementing the new plan required, of course, getting management to buy the idea. Then IS had to be taught to support the facilitator role, providing ways to help facilitators get IS services to users. One important contribution that IS made was developing more documentation like problem-solving guides and lists of qualified training resources to back up the people in the departments who would now be doing front-line support.

The facilitator had the key role in the new arrangement. Early on, that person had to assess the present computer knowledge of the unit's members, identify likely mentors, and begin augmenting the mentors' skills through tailored training. A seminar was developed to prepare facilitators for their new roles, covering some of the following topics.

- How strategic advantage can be gained from computer technology

- Cost and value of technology assets

- Liabilities involved with the technology, including guidelines for computer security

- Role of users in implementing technology

As more units at Corning begin to adopt the user resource network concept, consultant Braverman says, a question has arisen as to how "technical" the role of the facilitator should be. Since the main responsibilities are really managerial, the need for a technological guru in this role may not be primary.

Corning has been happy with the results of the program and is currently phasing it into other departments. Users find support is closer to hand, more personal, and quicker. The fact that the people who provide support are intimately aware of how the technology is being used is obviously a big plus. The gurus benefit because they're now acknowledged for the extra work they do and they're backed up with more resources. IS is happy because it's been freed from handling many "trivial" calls and can now concentrate on more strategic projects.

How well this kind of peer support network would work in other workplaces is a complex question. As Braverman and Hartwig point out in a *Computerworld* article (April 23, 1990), there must be a buy-off from IS and the business unit, a willingness to experiment, and a management sponsor willing to take risks. I would add: don't skip or shortchange the initial information gathering and brainstorming sessions.

Look closely at the level of computer experience in your organization, how evenly it is distributed between departments, and how much users are already helping other users. What you absolutely don't want to do is create a situation where you've stolen productive working time from staff and added support and training duties that could be done more economically by specialists. Peer support is no panacea, but it has a lot of potential in some organizations when it's carefully thought through and implemented, as it was at Corning.

Outsourcing Support

Maybe your organization shouldn't be in the computer support business at all. You could hire out all or part of your support responsibilities to a specialized service bureau like the one I work for. "Outsourcing" has become a buzzword lately, referring, of course, to procuring various services from outside vendors instead of maintaining internal infrastructure and staff. Many organizations are accustomed to paying an outside company to take on computer hardware maintenance duties, and Kodak recently made news by hiring IBM to run its whole MIS operation. Yet the idea of paying outsiders to answer your company's help calls may be a less familiar, even alien concept. A number of companies are working to change that unfamiliarity into widespread acceptance.

Third-party support companies promise to answer subscribers' hardware and software questions just as an internal help desk would. Pioneers in the field include specialized service companies like MSR in Atlanta and Computer Hand Holding in San Francisco, my company. A number of nationwide retailers have hotline service offerings. Recently the biggest player of them all, IBM, has entered the fray with their End-User Support program. Most of these companies determine their monthly fees by multiplying the number of employees who'll be eligible to call by a dollar amount. The rate is likely to be lower as the number of eligible callers increases. Some service providers sell blocks of calls—so many calls for a certain amount of money.

Should a conscientious organization pay someone else to help its employees when they have trouble? Since I'm directly involved in a company that provides third-party support I might not be completely objective on the subject so I won't try to cover both sides of the argument myself. I'll list some of the arguments for outsourcing and then turn to Cheryl Currid, *PC Week* columnist, to give another perspective.

Let's start with the pros.

Cost. Hiring third-party support might be cheaper for many organizations than providing it themselves. If one help desk person is supporting 100 users, one percent of his salary is attributable to one user's needs. That one percent might easily be $500 per year per supported user, including benefits. That's more than several of the third-party support companies would charge to handle one user's problems for a year. Add to the cost of the inhouse support person's salary that of normal overhead, and you may decide that outsourcing represents an economical alternative. Outsourcing support also means that someone else has absorbed the cost of training the support staff.

Leverage. Smaller organizations may well find that third-party support is the only way to provide adequate help to their users. How many shops with less than a couple of hundred PCs are able to staff adequately to handle the range of problems that users experience? Third-party support would mean that smaller organizations would have access to well-trained experts in any of the popular products.

Flexibility. For companies that already have help desks, third-party support can provide the flexibility to cover temporary increases in demand without hiring new people. Most information centers are under sharp constraints on "head count" these days and may find it preferable to pay for outside support that can be shut off later if demand slackens.

Focus. Many companies find third-party support attractive because they want to concentrate on more "strategic" aspects of technology than staffing and operating a help desk. They want their precious managerial expertise devoted to projects that are going to pay off more dramatically.

Now here's Cheryl Currid with another perspective on outsourcing support.

> I believe most large organizations are better off with inhouse teams rather than outsourcing. My reasons for that include:
>
> * Inhouse teams are usually cheaper than outsourcing, if you have over 250 to 500 units.
>
> * An inhouse computer service provides some opportunity for a career path for individuals.
>
> * Inhouse teams can provide higher service levels (assuming they are adequately staffed).
>
> * There is a strategic value to having your own talent. This is especially true in the early days of building a corporate connectivity platform. Company employees are generally more loyal and more willing to take on extra work. *TUNED IN TO COMPANY CULTURE*
>
> Given all that, I believe outsourcing is appropriate for other situations. In smaller companies, for example, it might be difficult to recruit the talent to make up the right team. Also, the cost equation tends to shift. It could be more cost effective to rent rather than buy your own talent in a smaller company.

Ms. Currid and I agree that smaller organizations may well find a lot of reasons to outsource, though we differ about the economics of the proposition for larger ones, and about service levels. What she says about some of the side benefits of inhouse support is very interesting. There are definitely many aspects of the decision that go beyond strictly dollars and cents issues.

Third-party support has not, it's fair to say, been an easy sale up to now, and it may be largely because of those less quantifiable aspects—issues such as control of quality, fear that outsiders won't follow company procedures, and protection of info center turf. No doubt some users would prefer not to deal with outsiders when they're in trouble, though many others don't seem to mind at all as long as the service is good and the answers correct. There may even be advantages to having an outside perspective. Yet there may be times when the outsider's lack of specific knowledge of the client company's procedures and applications can be a problem, and so can the fact that hotline support may not always be what's needed. An inhouse support operation will often have an easier time solving a problem by visiting the user and taking a look at what's happening. Because of this, third-party support companies are increasingly finding it important to be able to do house calls when the telephone isn't enough.

The biggest question of all is quality. How well does a third-party support outfit do at helping their customers? They may have some advantages over inhouse staffs—support is their full-time business, after all—and if they're not good they probably won't survive. They may have more extensive information resources than most help desks can offer.

Whether or not an organization decides to try the third-party option, looking closely at the question can be a valuable exercise. Try to objectively assess how good a job your company is doing in supporting its users. Figure out what it's costing to support each user and then ask some of the support companies what they would charge. Ask to sample their services and find out if they're willing to adapt to the way your company operates. Then think hard about what would be lost and what gained if you no longer had to answer those questions yourself.

The third-party tech support industry is small and very young, so it's likely to evolve considerably in the years to come, but it's already a significant alternative that's worth a second look.

Help for Nonprofits Some small organizations—even some not-so-small ones—may not be able to afford inhouse support or the third-party variety. I'm talking about the thousands of nonprofit organizations that foster everything from art to zoology, and often do it on a fraying shoestring. Realizing that computers could multiply their effectiveness, nonprofits may find a way to squeeze a few PCs into their budgets, but they're rarely able to field sufficient support personnel to keep up with installation, training, troubleshooting, and help desk needs.

Luckily, help is on the way in the form of—you guessed it—other nonprofits. Support organizations devoted strictly to helping with nonprofits' computer needs have grown up in the past few years. Though what these nonprofit support organizations do often goes beyond technical support, extending to providing consulting, training, systems design, and programming, they do fill a fundamental tech support role as well.

Some of these nonprofit support groups charge modest fees for their services. Others live on foundation grants entirely. Some are called "technology assistance centers," and provide a range of resources to nonprofits.

Another approach is exemplified by the CompuMentor Project based in San Francisco. Formed in 1986, this organization links up computer-savvy volunteers with nonprofits that need help. The help is usually in the form of training, but once a connection is made between a mentor and a nonprofit, that mentor might provide a range of support, from advising on what products to buy, to creating applications, to solving technical problems over the telephone.

The CompuMentor Project has adopted a powerful online tool to help it recruit mentors to assist specific nonprofits. An ongoing conference on the WELL (Whole Earth 'Lectronic Link) computer network functions as a medium for communication between CompuMentor staff and the technically astute population it relies on. The WELL's friendly and low-cost electronic milieu is perfect for CompuMentor's purposes. By posting the needs of specific nonprofits in some detail, CompuMentor gives the gurus a chance to see which organizations are most in need of their particular expertise and most in line with their interests and values. The WELL also serves as a place for CompuMentor staff to pass along specific questions and problems to a technically knowledgeable community. Anyone who logs onto the WELL might provide an answer to a nonprofit's technical questions without taking on the long-term relationship that compumentoring usually entails.

To date, the San Francisco CompuMentor Project has helped almost 400 nonprofits by linking them up with nearly 600 mentors. The group provides information for people interested in starting similar projects in other cities, and a number of them have taken root. For nonprofits doing important work without many resources, the kind of support compumentoring provides is invaluable, and the people who volunteer their time and skills get some significant satisfaction.

Insider Aiding

Computer users need help if they're going to get any work done. As more and more important business computing functions are being carried out on the desktop instead of in the glass house, and as the technology becomes more complex, the need for skilled support services grows. Yet the difficulty of quantifying that need makes it hard to withstand management pressure to pare down support staffs to a minimum.

Support managers have to fight, organizing their operations as efficiently as possible, choosing the right people and treating them right, and arming themselves with as much information as possible to prove the value of the help they provide. Support staffs have to maintain a strong service orientation, giving their internal customers the same kind of attention the company gives to its external customers.

Alternatives like peer support and outsourcing are emerging. Most likely they'll augment rather than replace more traditional modes. Creative initiatives are developing to help users outside the walls of corporations. In the long run, internal support is bound to evolve into new forms as it's integrated with training and consulting, taking on a wider view of what users need to make them more productive.

Communication Skills

For tech support people, communication skills are at least as important as technical knowledge and problem-solving ability. You need to listen carefully and speak clearly and confidently, creating a relationship with the caller that encourages cooperation and trust. You have to convey respect for the caller and represent your organization professionally. It's often hard—you're likely to deal with people who are frustrated, angry, impatient, even sometimes abusive. You may feel pressure to complete calls as quickly as possible even though your callers demand a lot of time and attention.

In this chapter we'll focus on the human dimension of hotline support. We'll explore ways to satisfy the needs of the caller and the support person for constructive, positive communication to solve technical problems. We'll also explore ways to satisfy the need of the support organization to be as efficient as possible with expensive talk-time. We'll look at skills that work to establish rapport with callers, explore techniques that help with problem calls, and cover basic hotline etiquette. Before getting down to specifics, though, let's deal with a few general issues.

Communication skills can be improved. Most of us think we're quite competent to talk on the telephone—after all, we've been doing it regularly since the age of 12 or younger. We may also consider ourselves good communicators, and we've developed a bag of tricks for dealing with different types of people. Chances are, if we've chosen support work, we *are* already good at dealing with people. Yet after spending some time doing hotline support we may find that many calls just don't go right. Tempers flair, the callers' and our own. We may have to repeat ourselves too often, or perhaps the caller seems more interested in telling his life story than hearing our technical advice. Calls may take much longer than they should. Ultimately, support people may face job burnout from the recurring stress of difficult interactions. Is it possible to build on our already well-developed communication skills to deal with the common problems of support work?

There are some important and easily learned techniques that can improve telephone communication considerably. Research by psychologists and communication experts has produced some valuable practical advice. I've found particularly useful the work of Dr. Gary S. Goodman, whose book *Winning by Telephone* (Prentice-Hall, 1982) will help anyone who spends much time on the phone for a living.

Better communication is self-defense. Most support organizations spend very little time training their employees in the art of telephone communication. The commonplace nature of the telephone may obscure the need for skill and technique in using it, and the importance of technical knowledge may outweigh other training needs.

Yet the work we do when dealing with people's problems on the phone is unusually difficult. Customer service authority Karl Albrecht calls it "emotional labor." "Emotional labor is any kind of work where the employee's *feelings* are in some ways the tools of his or her trade" (*Service Within*, Dow Jones-Irwin, 1990). When you do this kind of work you're in contact with one person after another with little control of the work flow. You have to cope with the customer's distress and respond positively, and the distress may end up rubbing off on you. There's even a name for it—"contact overload syndrome." I believe that paying more attention to the way you talk and listen to your customers can reduce the stress and keep you fresh in this work much longer.

Communication skills, not "smile training." Support work is almost always done in the context of a customer service relationship, whether you're supporting a manufacturer's products or helping internal customers on a help desk. This means that the way you talk to your callers reflects on your organization as much as it reflects on you personally. Customers are as likely to form an opinion of your organization's service orientation on the basis of the *way* you talk as they are by *what* you say. Yet we don't want to do what some people disparage as "smile training," teaching ways to "stroke" customers without providing real solutions to their problems. Improving communication is intimately tied to better ways of solving the technical problems support people deal with everyday.

Controlling the Call

Most people don't like the feeling of being controlled by others, but they do appreciate dealing with someone who speaks with confidence and authority. Most people also respond favorably to skillful use of communication techniques that guide the interaction to a mutually satisfying conclusion in a reasonably short time. Organizations that offer tech support spend a lot of money for it. They should realize that they have a strong interest in fostering better communication. This is not "touchy-feely" stuff or "psychobabble," but a significant contribution to the bottom line, paying off in greater customer satisfaction, shorter support calls, and improved staff morale.

The distinction between trying to control the *caller* and controlling the *call* is very important. The former is a manipulative approach that attempts to use guile to influence someone without his conscious knowledge and consent. The latter is an up-front attempt to convey information in the clearest, most efficient way possible while paying attention to the feelings of the caller and the caller's need for respect, participation, and dignity. To control the call, as the tech you must learn to control your own behavior, whatever the caller chooses to do, and whatever the technical issues involved. At the same time, you must remain flexible and responsive to the person at the end of the line.

Controlling the call is something that both parties can do quite happily at the same time. Both the caller and you normally have primary goals that are mutually attainable—answers or solutions, the reporting of problems—and both can use communication techniques to achieve those goals expeditiously. I've often been amused to find that some callers use the same kinds of techniques I'm using to get what they need from me. This presents no problems. I'm not being manipulated and neither are they. We share the same goal—an efficient solution to a technical problem and a positive human interaction.

All is not sunshine and mutual respect on the tech support lines, however. In addition to the up-front goal of getting help for their technical problems, some callers have hidden goals, unknown to themselves, perhaps, that can really louse up a communication session if you aren't careful and prepared. Controlling the call in this case means quickly spotting the "hidden" agenda of the caller, devising strategies to cope with it, and carefully executing those strategies, while still paying attention to the technical issues. Coping with these kinds of difficult calls will be discussed later on. Right now we'll discuss the three factors in controlling calls—paying attention, setting the tone, and developing professional phone support relationships.

The Primary
Ingredient:
Attention

The most important factor in the success of the tech support interaction is the attention and involvement of the support person. Repeatedly, I've found that I can handle the most difficult technical problems and the most difficult people when I'm paying full attention to the matter at hand, listening carefully to the words and tone of the caller and letting my mind fully engage in the technical problem being presented. On the other hand, when I've been distracted by outside events or my own preoccupations, I've found routine calls can bog down and take forever to complete, and small misunderstandings can lead to anger and frustration.

Technical support is done in "real time," like baseball or ballet, and as in those activities, preparation and training is only the prelude to a successful performance. Robert Kausen, in his useful book, *Customer Satisfaction Guaranteed* (Life Education, 1989), points to the quality of presence as key to success in dealing with customers. Presence is "the state of giving your full attention to the matter at hand." The enemy of presence is distraction, both from within and outside. Letting go of internal distractions and reducing external ones (like colleagues talking right next to your workstation) are the first key steps in developing the presence and attention necessary to do tech support right.

Kausen points to involvement as the ultimate expression of presence. The greater the involvement of the representative, the greater the satisfaction of the customer and the greater the pleasure of the representative in the work. In my experience, callers have generally expressed more appreciation for my attention to them and their problems than for efficient technical solutions. Below are some tips for increasing presence and attention.

Create the best possible physical environment for work. Ideally, employees should be involved in the design and arrangement of their own work areas. Do what you can to remove physical distractions and sources of discomfort. Find equipment that works well and is adaptable to different people. Get comfortable furniture!

Imagine the caller as a real person. It's much easier to pay attention to a real person than just a disembodied voice. At Computer Hand Holding, we record the caller's name and phone number first, which gives an opportunity to form a picture of a real person in a real city. It's interesting and involving to listen to the quality of the caller's voice, choice of words, and pace, in addition to the words themselves. Asking how the caller is using the product in his work can heighten your sense of involvement.

Be aware of your internal distractions and let go of them. What kinds of thoughts recur as you answer tech support calls? Are there fears or concerns that keep distracting you from the matters at hand? Are there technical areas where you don't feel confident, or company policies that you don't understand completely or don't feel comfortable with? Do you feel pressure to answer all calls within a certain length of time? Are there personal issues that compete for your attention? Jotting down these kinds of thoughts for later attention might help free you from worrying about them when you're on the phone and allow more complete attention to callers.

Don't work beyond your limits. Taking call after call without a break almost invariably leads to diminished attention. Tech support requires pretty intense concentration, and few people can sustain it for long stretches without a break. When you take a break, get away from your workstation, if possible, and don't think about computers until you come back (unless that's what refreshes you).

Setting the Tone   The first few seconds set the tone for the rest of the call, whether the greeting is electronic or human, or whether there is a call-routing system or direct contact with the technical support.

The electronic hello. The first impression the caller gets of the tech support operation may be of an answering machine or call-routing system. I'm amazed how often that recorded voice is cold and officious, lacking in any warmth or friendliness. If callers are queued and left on hold, they're often subjected to music they

would never choose or to local radio stations complete with commercials. No wonder folks are often irritated by the time they get through. If you have anything to do with choosing how the answering and call-routing systems in your organization are set up, put a lot of thought into it. Find someone in your organization who can speak clearly and professionally, and still sound human. Pick hold music that has a little character—nothing extreme but not the kind of stuff you hear in elevators. Think about ways to make life more pleasant for the folks that have to be on hold for a while. At WordPerfect Corporation, they've recently introduced "Hold Disk Jockeys," real human beings that play music and monitor the caller queues, announcing periodically how long the average wait time is, even telling individual callers that they are going to be getting help soon. It's a luxury most of us can't match, but it's a good example of paying attention to callers' first impressions and communicating that you want to help them.

Scripting calls for better communication. Once a caller's off hold and in your hands, you need to answer the phone, greet the caller, and tell him that you want to help. You have to give him a positive and accurate impression of who you are and invite him to explain what he needs.

A support organization needs to streamline the call-taking process while still treating callers and support reps as individuals. It must also ensure that callers are given a positive impression of the organization and that different encounters with it are uniformly professional and courteous.

One tool for achieving these goals is the answering script, a written protocol for support reps to follow in answering calls. If you want to see how elaborate scripting can become, listen carefully the next time a sophisticated telemarketer calls you up. He is likely to follow a carefully designed script with prewritten and rehearsed responses to many of the "customer's" potential objections to making the purchase. People make a lot of money writing these scripts. Given the great variety of technical support calls, and the fact that we're not trying to sell anybody anything, there's no need for us to go to these lengths to thoroughly script calls, but there's plenty of reason to work out effective greetings that start things out efficiently and convey the organization's commitment to the customer.

Basically, what's needed is to identify the organization and the individual support person, to declare the fact that the caller has reached help, and to ask the caller for whatever is needed from him at the outset. There are many approaches to opening greetings and it's a place for an organization to express its identity. At Computer Hand Holding we've evolved the following simple script.

"Hello, this is the Computer Hand Holding tech support line. My name is Ralph. May I have your name please?"

Caller gives name.

"Thank you. May I have your area code and phone number?" Caller supplies it.

"Thanks. How may I help you?"

This is not academy award scriptwriting, but it does get the job done. We document all calls so we need to get the caller to supply his name and phone number. We found that if we didn't ask for it right away many callers would launch into their problems, and a lot of time could go by before we could interrupt and ask for the information we needed to start logging the call. Since we measure the length of calls and use that timing in several ways, we wanted it to be accurate.

We found that giving the support person's name at the top seemed to make it easier for the caller to give his name. In this security-conscious age, many organizations have stopped giving out employees' full names, which is unfortunate but probably sensible. I would prefer giving the full name as an indicator of personal commitment and pride, but safety comes first. By the way, very few callers refuse to give their names and phone numbers, or even seem hesitant to give them.

Answer calls in a cheerful, positive tone without sounding "fake." The knack of sounding consistently cheerful and positive is not easy, but it can be learned and it really helps the communication process. Bear in mind that most people who call a hotline are in some kind of stress and appreciate a friendly, service-oriented person on the other end of the line. Perhaps the easiest trick for cultivating this tone is to practice the opening script and develop one's own, honest way to say the words, "How may I help you?" or the equivalent. What kind of voice do *you* want to hear when you need help? Work on trying to sound that way. Get over the shock of hearing your own voice and use a tape recorder to find out how you sound to others during your opening lines.

During the course of the workday, fatigue and stress may lead to a change in your tone, perhaps even allowing a slightly hostile "edge" to creep into your voice. After a series of difficult calls, it's natural for an internal voice to cry out, "Why do they keep bothering *me* with their problems!" This can lead to a vicious circle, with callers responding negatively to the negative tone and calls becoming more stressful for both parties. The obvious organizational solution is to improve the work situation for tech support people by varying tasks, getting time off the phone for training and research, taking real breaks away from the phones, and getting some exercise. But to keep on top of one's own communication, it's important not to "go on automatic pilot." It's essential to continue to pay attention throughout the day to how our voices sound and how others are responding to them, and to make adjustments as necessary.

One point needs to be emphasized here. Although cheerful, friendly, positive voices do win friends and influence people, these qualities should not be faked or affected. Unnaturally cheerful voices turn off many people because they sound dishonest or inappropriate to problem-solving situations.

Developing Professional Phone Support Relationships

Paying attention throughout the call and setting the tone for the first impression go a long way to helping you control a call successfully. But a greater challenge lies in controlling the call while resolving the technical problem. The key is to develop phone support relationships. Let's examine ways to accomplish that.

Develop a professional and respectful but informal style. Most people respond well to a style that combines warmth with professionalism. Callers want to deal with competent human beings, with equal emphasis on competent *and* human. They also want to be treated with respect, which means, in this context, being treated as a valued customer. They differ considerably as to how formal or informal they prefer to be with people they don't know, how much small talk they like to engage in, and how fast they like to talk.

The tech support person will get valuable clues about how a caller wants to be spoken to by listening to the first few words of the conversation. Does the person give his first name? A title (Dr. Brown, Mr. Black)? Speak quickly or slowly? Does the person say something like, "How you doing today?" or speak in carefully measured phrases? These kinds of clues should give a sense of how to make the caller feel more comfortable, and thereby make the call proceed more smoothly. I'm not suggesting that we should be chameleons, mimicking the style of the caller without regard for our own preferences, but rather that we need to develop the flexibility to adapt comfortably to different interactive styles. People tend to feel more comfortable when you mirror them to some extent, offering some reflection of their style. Learning to deal with people on this level requires a certain amount of playfulness as well as sensitivity. It can contribute to a tech support person's feeling of fun and skill in his work. It will also reduce the number of frustrating, unsatisfying calls.

Develop the quality of empathy for the caller's situation. Closely related to a positive tone of voice is a quality of honest concern and fellow-feeling that shows the caller you're on his side. Empathy may be the most important interpersonal quality in a tech, or anyone in a service profession, because it fosters a spirit of cooperative enterprise between two parties that defuses potential hostility and insecurity. It inspires optimism and trust, since the caller no longer feels alone with the problem. From your perspective, empathy helps focus attention on the caller's point of view, which may lead to better troubleshooting and clearer explanations. Empathy also motivates, allowing you to go the extra mile to find a solution.

Empathy is not a matter of stock responses, but it can be communicated to the caller through simple phrases.

"I understand."

"I see what you mean."

"That's a very tough problem. I think we can work it out, though."

"Boy, that sounds terrible!"

"I can see why you're upset."

"I know the manual isn't completely clear on that."

"Thanks for your patience."

One technique used by counselors is quite useful in tech support work. It's called "active listening," and it involves responding to what you're being told with a summary in your own words of what you understand to be the message. It takes some practice to do this smoothly, and it isn't always appropriate, but it can be very useful in both sorting out technical issues and communicating your effort to understand what's being said.

Caller: "When I tried to pop up your program my computer went totally bonkers and now there's all sorts of garbage all over my screen and I can't get my program back."

Tech: "Your screen got messed up when you popped us up and you can't restore it. Let me ask you a few questions..."

By repeating the key elements you give the caller time to pause and feel that on the other end of the line you understand and are trying to help.

The emphasis is on shared concern and a sense that the support person is attuned to the caller's point of view. There's also an acknowledgement that though technical problems are the subject at hand, there's a human dimension that needs to be addressed as well.

One common obstacle to empathy that plagues tech support people is the fact that we are often dealing with callers who seem confused, stressed, forgetful, foolish, or, occasionally, downright stupid. A large percentage of callers have not read their documentation, don't know much about computers, and have blocks that prevent them from learning about them. Despite their discomfort, many of these people have had to become computer users at their jobs and have become fairly competent at one or two software packages, though they are quickly lost when they venture beyond. But technical support people are usually quite different. They love the technology or at least like it, and they may well spend time tinkering and learning just for the fun of it. They enjoy the feeling of mastery that a deeper understanding brings. It may be hard for such people to develop empathy for the less-adept callers who have to be led slowly and carefully through every procedure. One tech support person often says half-seriously after such a call, "Computer users should have to pass a test!"

Perhaps the solution to this dilemma is simply to reflect that there are areas where each of us is lost, helpless, and in need of some patient hand-holding, whether it be in a hospital, automotive shop, or counselor's office. And there are probably times when each of us has lapses of foolishness or even stupidity. We can only hope then that an empathetic helper will be available to see us through.

Get the caller's name right and use it carefully. Most people take their names very seriously and don't like them clobbered. At the beginning of the call when you invite the caller to identify himself, ask the caller to spell the name and make sure you enter it correctly in your logging system (if you use one). Even "Smith" has alternate spellings. Don't make comments about names that are "strange" or "foreign." The question of whether to call people by their first names, use Mr. or Ms., or avoid names in direct address entirely is a little tricky. Some people communicate such informality that you know they will be happiest with their first names. When you get no such indication, the safe thing is to use Mr., Ms., Dr., and the last name or "Sir" or "Ma'am." No one will be offended by that. But the point is, whenever you can use the appropriate form of address during the call, do so. It adds to the human dimension and overall satisfaction for you and the caller.

A little small talk goes a long way. Purposely ambiguous, this heading indicates the two-edged nature of small talk in the context of tech support calls. It may serve a valuable function, but it's not something to be done to excess. Your time is valuable and so is the caller's. You both need to maximize the efficiency of that time by focusing on the technical problems the caller needs help with. But a moment or two spent asking what the weather is like in Memphis or how the caller likes the new computer he is using can be a relaxing way to develop some rapport and keep from burning out. A special form of small talk is humor, which can improve the problem-solving process or else fall totally flat. Take your cue from the caller's style.

Speak confidently. Just as airline passengers and surgical patients want to hear calm, confident voices from the people they're about to entrust with their lives, callers want a sense of confidence to be communicated by the person who's trying to get them out of a technical mess. We expect that the confident-sounding voice goes with the knowledge and skill to back it up, and we're more likely to listen to, trust, and follow the advice of someone who sounds like he knows what he's doing, even when he admits that he doesn't have all the answers.

Confidence should start with a sense of one's knowledge of the technical product being supported and the environments it is designed to work in. As a tech support person, you need to continuously reinforce your knowledge by filling in gaps and communicating with others who are a source of help and information. At least as important as technical knowledge, knowledge of company policies and procedures, both written and unwritten, is crucial to confidently help people with your company's products. A well-founded belief in your organization, its integrity, and the quality of its products should help inspire confidence in you as you support those products.

But confidence is not solely based on knowledge, competence, and belief in one's organization. It also rests on a personal sense of self-worth and self-trust, which are communicated to others on the phone by the vocal qualities we use. Some people come by a confident voice easily and others do not, but it can be attained through attention and practice. Use a tape recorder to check whether your voice is tentative or strong, calm or flustered. There are many books which offer advice for improving the quality of the spoken voice, and many speech experts who can help. A confident voice is a great asset, worth devoting time and attention to.

Here are some tips for developing a confident approach to answering questions.

• When you have the answer to the caller's problem, give it clearly and as succinctly as possible in language you've gauged to suit the caller's level of expertise.

• Cite the product documentation when appropriate, and work at developing clear answers for commonly asked questions.

- When asking questions to diagnose a problem, have a goal in mind. Try not to sound as if you're clutching at straws (even when you are). Keeping a list of useful diagnostic questions handy helps greatly.

- Try to get rid of "you knows," "likes," "I guesses," and other such empty phrases. They don't communicate confidence or knowledgeability.

- Avoid a rising inflection at the end of statements that may sound like self-doubt instead of self-confidence.

- Pause occasionally, even within a sentence, to think through the problem. Pausing gives you time to plan your trouble-shooting strategy and to choose your words more carefully so you don't have to repeat yourself.

- Don't be embarrassed by not knowing the answer right away. Say something like, "That's a tough one, unique as far as I know. Let me ask you a few more questions."

- Develop a smooth, confident way to say you need to escalate or research the problem. This may be difficult for people who are proud of their technical knowledge. Learn to say something like, "I'll have to do some research and get back to you. I should be able to get back by tomorrow morning (or whenever)." Of course, make sure you meet all such commitments, if only to say that more time will be necessary.

- Don't be defensive about the product's possible shortcomings, even if the caller tries to link you personally with them. Much of such criticism is unfair, but since you are the one the caller can blame, you sometimes have to take the heat. Remember, though you do represent your company, you don't need to take personal responsibility for everything done by your organization.

- Be truthful. Honesty is a great policy for many reasons, not least because dishonesty undermines one's own sense of self-worth and confidence. By avoiding telling callers anything that's not true, you keep yourself on solid ground. Honesty is crucial to maintaining your organization's ethical and legal position as well. Note, though, that being honest doesn't mean that every question must be answered. There may be many business reasons why an organization would choose not to answer certain questions about its products. Saying clearly that the company doesn't reveal certain information is the honest and ethical way to deal with such situations.

Avoid stereotypes. No one, alas, is free from prejudices and stereotypes, whether racial, national, regional, sexual, political, or religious. It's crucial, though, that people in service occupations like tech support learn to treat everyone fairly and without prejudice. Assumptions about the intelligence or "goodness" of a caller made on the basis of his ethnic group, nationality, region, or sex usually lead to serious breakdowns in communication.

Adjust to nonnative English speakers. Don't talk down to them. Imagine trying to discuss computer problems in a foreign language. Pretty tough. Make it easier on callers whose native language isn't English by speaking carefully, avoiding colloquialisms, and showing patience. Don't speak v-e-r-y s-l-o-w-l-y. Don't be impatient.

Dealing with Difficult Calls

Difficult calls occur for any number of reasons and can sidetrack the most experienced support people. This section offers suggestions for handling the hazards of corporate bureaucracy, complaints, anger, abuse, novice users, sceptics, the silent type, and the nonstop talker.

Shortcutting the Runaround

In dealing with people who feel that they have been given a runaround by your organization or by technology in general, it's important to minimize further frustration as much as possible. This might mean shortcutting any further steps necessary to resolve problems so the caller doesn't get shunted to yet another department or service person.

The issues of whether the caller is "right or wrong" or whether the problem is strictly a technical support question are much less important than resolving a problem that might lead to repeated calls, product returns, bad "word of mouth" about your company, and a loss of future business from the caller. Make sure that you follow through completely with such problems to avoid giving the caller yet another runaround. Your organization should have functioning escalation policies to deal with problems that are beyond your authority to solve. Do what you can to get your callers' problems taken care of by knowing the policies and following them.

Dealing with Complaints

When a caller is angry about a perceived shortcoming in your company's product, whether it be a bug, a design feature, or a compatibility or performance issue, your desire to defend your company's products is as natural as the caller's need to complain, but as a professional your primary responsibility is to take in the feedback the caller offers, explain policy or the way the product works, acknowledge bugs, and offer solutions.

It's important to remember that any complex technical product is a result of hundreds of design decisions and compromises and thousands of chances for problems. What one user calls a feature, another might consider a bug. And then there are the plain, uncontroversial bugs. The upshot is that not everyone is going to be happy with the design and performance of your company's product, and that there will probably be bugs and problems found and suggestions offered for improvement.

Avoid defensiveness. It's much better to portray yourself and your company as willing to learn about and correct problems and to welcome suggestions than as incapable of making mistakes. Feedback from users should be treated as a precious commodity, recorded carefully and passed on to those in a position to evaluate and respond to it. When this is the policy, the caller with a complaint or suggestion can be honestly thanked for his feedback and most often will have a sense of satisfaction about being listened to.

Dealing with Anger

"I'm mad as Hell and I'm not going to take it anymore!" Nothing is more harrowing for most tech support people than answering a call and finding out that the caller is already boiling, either because of some drawn-out, frustrating scenario with your product or company, or because of some personal problems, work pressure, or just a plain nasty personality. Some people were born angry while others have anger thrust upon them.

Most people, even when frustrated and angry, will avoid personally abusing someone they're calling for help, but some know no bounds and use foul language and personal abuse freely. In my experience answering thousands of calls I can remember only a few who were personally insulting or abusive. But many more were so caught up in their anger that they were difficult to help, and, of course, many of these had difficult technical problems in the first place.

The skills mentioned so far in this chapter such as positive tone, empathetic response, and confident voice are all important in dealing with angry or upset callers, perhaps more than ever, but some cautions are in order and some special approaches are warranted. A positive and friendly tone, for example, must be a little different when dealing with an angry person. "Friendly" in this context means "willing to work things out." It would be silly

and possibly provocative to try to ignore the angry tone your caller is using. Empathy is very important, and can be communicated with phrases like these below.

"Sounds like you've had a hard time and I'm sorry. Let's see if we can work it out for you."

"I can understand your being angry. May I ask you a few questions about your system?"

Words like these usually go a long way toward calming angry people when they're accompanied by competent action to solve problems. They defuse confrontation without either party losing face. Angry people have a simple need to express their feelings, and the tech support person will have to sit tight while the complaints are being expressed, and then acknowledge the anger and start the process of attempting to solve the problem.

Dealing with Four-letter Abuse

Some people, luckily very few, don't just get mad when they have technical problems with a product, they turn into Genghis Khans! Spouting personal and corporate abuse, threatening lawsuits, using foul language, they generally try to ruin your day. You don't have to let them! It's important to remember that you have options in dealing with abusive or extremely angry people, that you are not at their mercy, and that you remain safe and secure regardless of a caller's ranting. Your options range from swearing back and hanging up (admittedly extreme), to putting the caller on hold "until they cool off," to passing a call to a supervisor, to using your interpersonal skills to defuse the situation and deal with the caller's complaint. Only the last solution significantly adds to a sense of mastery and professional satisfaction.

Basically, you have two positive options in dealing with harsh and abusive language: ignore it or politely ask the caller to refrain from such language if possible. Choosing to ignore the harsh language has the advantage of being entirely within your control, and in some cases the caller will simply calm down once he realizes that the language will not get your goat. Asking for a change risks further angering the caller, but if done properly may remind some callers that they are dealing with human beings and that they might get better service if they cool the invective.

Each of us has habitual responses to dealing with angry people, habits that began forming very early in our lives. Gary Goodman, in *Winning by Telephone*, suggests there are five common negative responses that get in the way of successful outcomes: avoidance, withdrawal, denial, compromise, and retaliation. The trick for the service person who has to deal with the abusive caller is to maintain a respectful approach throughout the transaction and avoid sinking to the level of responding to the venom.

Here are some more tips for dealing with complaints and criticism.

Use active listening. Active listening (described earlier in this chapter) will help you get the gist of the criticisms and show that you are making an effort to understand.

Locate the crux of the matter. Identify the key insult, misunderstanding, or failure that may have put the transaction with this caller on the wrong track. Is there anything that can be done to alleviate the problem?

Conscientiously record the criticisms. As you would for any other feedback, take notes and make sure that they are passed along to someone in a position to evaluate them. Unpleasant as the caller is, the information is valuable. Taking the feedback seriously helps the tech support person deal with the caller respectfully.

Don't take personal offense. If the caller has criticisms of you, the tech support person, offer him an opportunity to talk to someone in a supervisory position. This should be done in a neutral, open way. It helps to have a good supervisor.

Dealing with Novice Users and the Terminally Confused

"What do you mean 'reboot?' I've never kicked it at all!" Though not as hair-raising as angry callers, novice or less than fully-trained computer users can be at least as frustrating for the tech support person. Although you may be quite competent to explain a product's intricacies and solve technical problems with assurance, communicating the most fundamental steps in hardware or software operations to someone with little computer experience can be trying and stressful. Suddenly the basic vocabulary you rely on to explain matters to more skilful users may be useless. Instead of talking about the "A: drive" you may have to physically describe an opening in the computer unit. Beyond this, there may be diagnostic questions to be answered to solve a problem and novice users may not provide reliable answers.

Two policy questions are important here. First, what level of skill does your company set as being the minimum required for a caller to receive tech support? Second, to what extent are you under pressure to keep calls short? If there is a company policy, stated clearly, that only people at a certain level of computer skill will be supported by help lines, you will have authority to avoid the most burdensome types of calls involving the most basic kinds of computer questions. There will still be a need for diplomatically explaining the policy to novice users, perhaps recommending a direction for the caller to receive needed instruction or suggesting that the caller get help from someone else within his organization.

The issue of how much pressure the tech support person feels to keep calls below a certain length bears heavily on how you

will be able to deal with novice callers. Obviously, it takes longer to troubleshoot when each step must be exhaustively explained. If there is time pressure, this can lead to exasperation and anger on your part, a tendency to cut the call short, and consequent feelings of pressure on the part of the caller. This does not bode well for the successful completion of the call. Though average call length might be one measure of your productivity and one that is very easy to measure, it is very important that it not be overemphasized. A tech support person who takes a little longer on average to answer questions may be giving better explanations and winning more friends for the company than one who races to closure with little attention to the needs of the caller.

Even if there is a policy regarding minimum computer skill, there will always be a need to help people with a less-than-ideal level of computer training and experience. It might be good to remember that you have a role to play in extending the usefulness of computers and software beyond the core of dedicated techies, and that the health of the industry depends on this broadening. Here are some tips for communicating with people who lack high-tech skills but do have high-tech problems.

Maintain a reassuring, upbeat tone. Novice and seminovice callers often apologize for "not being very smart at this stuff." Tell them they're doing fine or that they'll soon be computer consultants. After they successfully complete a step, say "Great!" or something encouraging. You want your callers to gain confidence in themselves and in you.

Avoid jargon. Every industry has its share of terminology that insiders use freely but outsiders find impenetrable, and the computer industry is particularly jargon-happy. Try to gauge the technical expertise of your caller and choose your words accordingly. With novices you often need to describe procedures rather than use computer jargon. Say "Hold down the shift key and the print screen key," rather than "Do a screen dump."

Don't give your caller more information than he can handle. Check often to make sure you're being understood.

Break up explanations into small chunks. Ask questions like, "Do you know what I mean when I say _____?" or "Are you with me so far?" You don't want to patronize but neither do you want a scared caller to go on without understanding for fear of sounding dumb, so give him plenty of chances to get clarification.

Describe processes carefully and in more than one way. You may have to be redundant, explaining things several times in different words to get the point across. Try very hard to avoid ambiguous language and double-check often that the caller is doing exactly what you think he is.

Avoid disaster. If you must talk a caller through a computer process, make sure to take steps to avoid destroying files by having the caller make backups or take other precautions first. If you have a feeling that the caller cannot be trusted to do something safely, don't continue with the process. Insist that he get some onsite help.

Follow along. No matter how well you know your products, it helps to do the operation yourself while you're talking your caller through it.

Summarize often. If there is a lot of material to cover in a call it's very easy for the caller to forget important information. Summarizing important points at the end of the call can reinforce learning and confirm that key points have been understood.

Avoid a pedantic tone. No one likes to be talked down to. Though you are the expert and you may be in the position of teaching, you don't have to sound superior or contemptuous.

Dealing with Skeptics

"That's not it, I'm sure." There's something about computer hardware and software that brings out the skeptic in many people. After all, it's impossible for most people to know what's really going on in that mess of silicon and code and yet we've become dependent on it all working right for us. When something goes wrong, there's often some doubt whether the cause is something we did wrong, the computer did wrong, or some diabolical combination of the two.

On top of these doubts about where problems are coming from, add the sense of skepticism and near-paranoia many people feel about the companies they deal with today. After years of negative experiences many people tend to doubt the honesty of any company's representative. And internal support people may find that their callers are just as skeptical of the advice the help desk gives.

Some people are just naturally skeptical. The result for tech support is that some callers doubt just about anything you say as you try to help them with their problems. You suggest a line of inquiry and their skepticism blocks you at every step. "No, it couldn't be that," they say. You can end up feeling you have to convince them of everything you say, not just find a solution to their technical problem. Sometimes, this doubting attitude is found in quite knowledgeable users who feel they know more than the tech support person. Or the doubter may be someone who can't admit that he might have made a mistake, as you're trying to suggest.

In dealing with perennial doubters I've found no simple solutions, but some approaches help. The first thing to do is realize that you've got a skeptic on your hands, take a deep breath, and remind yourself to relax. You might find yourself on an uphill climb in getting over the mountain of skepticism. Don't get into arguments with the caller. If you have a procedure to check and the caller doubts its value, you may need to say something like, "I understand what you're saying, but we need to eliminate this possibility first." On occasion, after facing a steady stream of doubt from a caller, I've resorted to asking them, "What do you think is going on?" This has sometimes led to good suggestions, but at least it gives the caller a chance to assert his ideas.

. . . .

Dealing with the Silent Type

"I've got a problem but I don't want to talk about it." People who don't like to talk can be more difficult than those who don't want to stop. Sometimes you seem to have to drag words out of callers' mouths. Maybe they're shy. Maybe they don't want to reveal the limitations of their knowledge. In any case, you need to draw them out a little to get the information you need. Here are some tips.

Use open-ended questions. Instead of yes/no questions, you may want to emphasize more open-ended ones to get the caller to talk, and point them to the specific area you need information about.

"What do you see happening on the screen?"

"What does the printer do when you hit Print Screen?"

Slow down a little. Some people seem to clam up because they're a little anxious. We may forget that calling tech support is an unfamiliar experience for some people. By slowing the pace of your speech a little, you might make the caller more comfortable.

Offer encouragement. When a laconic caller does open up a little, offer some reinforcement such as "Okay, good," or "That's interesting…"

. . . .

Getting to Goodbye   Everyone has the experience of dealing with people who just don't seem to know how to say goodbye, who draw out every conversation well beyond the time necessary to complete the business at hand. In the tech support business, these people are particularly difficult to deal with. You don't want to alienate them as customers but you probably have other people waiting for help. Most people try to abide by the unspoken rule that neither party will take much longer than necessary to complete a business call, so these callers stand out as unusually annoying and insensitive. Sometimes, the more you try to get rid of these folks the more tenaciously they persist. And, most frustrating, just as they seem to be about to finally hang up, some small issue arises which can send the call off onto another lengthy tangent.

Perhaps these people are lonely and need all the attention they can get. Perhaps they're insecure and want to extract the last ounce of reassurance before they go off to try the solution on their own. Perhaps they have a need to get their money's worth in the form of technical support. Whatever their reasons, these people challenge you to remain courteous and professional *and* to find the most graceful way to get to goodbye. There are no universal solutions to the problem of the nonstop talker, but here are some tips that should help.

Listen carefully for unresolved issues. If the caller is continuing to talk and you think the subject has been fully covered, maybe there is some unclear point. Ask if there is anything the caller needs clarified.

Give cues that indicate the conversation should be winding to a close. You can say something like, "That should solve the problem. Will you please try it and call back if you have any more problems." Choose words and inflections that lead to a graceful end to the conversation. Saying, "I'm sorry, but I have to go now," is the last resort, to be reserved for the very hardest cases. And it doesn't always work.

Make it clear you have no more information to impart. There are several ways to courteously make clear to a caller that you have no more to say. You can repeat the key points you've made as often as necessary. You can be silent once you've conveyed the information a few times, responding to questions but not starting new topics. Try not to "rise to the bait" of an unnecessary conversational gambit.

Use yes/no questions and answers. If you want to limit the verbiage in the call, try asking questions that have yes/no answers. Answer questions with a simple yes or no when it's possible to do so politely. More narrative answers lead to longer calls when the caller is inclined in that direction.

Relax. Your rising frustration can make some people more talkative, so take a deep breath and try to see the humor in the situation.

Getting Derailed Calls Back on Track

No matter how carefully you've worked at learning the skills described here and developing your own tricks for helping people with their problems on the phone, there are times when things go wrong. Tempers flare, your mind wanders, an offhand remark causes misunderstanding, both caller and tech support person get totally confused, an impasse develops, or the caller wants something you can't deliver. How can you get back on track toward a successfully completed call? Here are some tips.

Learn to pause to regain balance. It's okay to say, "Excuse me for a moment. I need to think this through." And it may be the best way to regain your composure when things get confused. You may need to put the person on hold momentarily, close your eyes, and take a few deep breaths.

Build islands of understanding. When the problem is mutual confusion, frequently summarizing the facts that you and the caller both agree on and understand is helpful. Stop the flow of new information periodically and summarize what's been established.

Call attention to the communication process. If you and the caller seem to be butting heads or otherwise failing to work cooperatively, it might be necessary to call attention to that fact in order to put things on the right track. Gary Goodman, in his book on telephone interaction mentioned earlier in this chapter, calls this process "metacommunication," (communication about communication) and points out that it's not without danger. If things aren't going well, pointing out the fact might make them worse. But there may be times when you simply have to say something like, "I'm sorry, sir, but I'm having a hard time because you're giving me information faster than I can process it. Please slow down and we'll take it step by step."

Don't be afraid to apologize. If you discover you've somehow offended the caller or inadvertently given incorrect information, it's appropriate to apologize and try to get back on track. Some people hate to apologize, but it's a time-tested way to get past a mistake and on to a solution. It doesn't really cost anything to say you've blown it, and it's very rare for a caller to fail to accept an honestly offered apology. As a representative of your organization you might also be doing it a big service if you apologized for its shortcomings and mistakes as well.

Hotline Etiquette

At this point we've looked at a number of techniques for better communication on the support hotline. What follows is a little different—some points of hotline etiquette. What constitutes "good manners" is always open to discussion, reflecting the culture and values of an organization or individual. Rather than being the last word on the subject, this list is intended as a starting point for support organizations to formulate their own approach.

- Learn your telephone system thoroughly so you don't "lose" calls when transferring, or putting people on hold. If telephone system behavior that's outside of your control interferes with calls, report it immediately.

- If you do lose a caller, or if you have a bad connection, call back immediately. This is a good reason to take the caller's name and number early in the call.

- Swallow food and drink before picking up the phone.

- Before putting someone on hold, give an *honest* assessment of how long the wait will be and, if longer than a couple of minutes, give the option of being called back. If the caller chooses to hold and the wait is longer than you anticipated, pick up the phone and tell the caller what's happening.

- Don't be more informal or familiar with the caller than he invites you to be.

- Don't rush the caller. Wait for the caller to hang up first.

- Don't communicate stress, frustration, or boredom.

- Don't "bad-mouth" other people, companies, or products.

- Thank the caller for calling and invite him to call again.

- Treat callers as valued customers.

Winning Friends and Influencing Callers

Doing support work requires a rare combination of human relations and technical skills. Even natural communicators can benefit from careful attention to the way they deal with the people who call for help. Practical techniques exist to help the communication process. Focusing on communication is not the same as "smile training," the adoption of a style that emphasizes "surface" rather than "service."

Treating people like valuable customers and intelligent human beings is at the core of real service and communication. Sometimes it's tough. People don't always treat us as we'd like, no matter what we do. Nevertheless, resourceful support people find ways to make the best of the situation, serve the customer, and take care of themselves as well.

Handling Support Calls

Now that we've taken a look at the interpersonal aspects of technical support it's time to get down to the nuts and bolts—the process of answering technical questions, taking user feedback, and troubleshooting. The communication skills mentioned in the previous chapter are used throughout the process and we'll have occasion to refer to them here from time to time. For now we'll focus on the other skills and techniques needed to handle the typical calls that come into a support center. We'll look at the different kinds of calls and offer suggestions about how to handle each one most efficiently.

Can these required skills be taught, or are they only the hard-won result of years of apprenticeship and practice, trial and error? Since the dawn of the industrial age, technical problem-solving skills have been valued but there was little understanding of how they could be taught. The age of computers has created an ever-growing demand for skilled problem-solvers, but by and large people still learn to handle the intellectual challenges of support work by doing it, with little training on the specific skills involved. Support people are often given a manual and a computer and told to learn the product. Then, after a week or two, they're on the phones. Over time they'll probably pick up the intellectual skills that make the whole process flow smoothly, but only after a lot of difficult support calls. It seems to me that the process of learning could be made less painful by some explicit attention to the thinking processes involved in support work.

Nothing in this chapter should suggest that tech support is a completely logical process or that it's simple and easily learned. There's plenty of room for old-fashioned hunch and inspiration, and like everywhere else in the universe, chaos has a way of entering the system now and then. We're going to describe a simplified model of tech support in order to find ways to make the day-to-day realities of the work a little more rational.

Supportthink

It's amazing that people can do support at all. You sit there plugged into a telephone headset, listening to people you've never met describing strange goings on in their computer systems. You're completely dependent on them to describe what's happening, but you know you can't trust everyone to describe things correctly. You have to imagine what's going on within a system that's extremely complicated and try to come up with tests and experiments that will lead to a solution to a problem you may never have heard before. And you have to do all of this within a fairly short time period to keep your employer and your caller happy. It's fantastic that the mind can handle these challenges as well as it does, but it would be nice if we could build on our natural brilliance a little.

Researchers in cognitive science and education don't seem to have come to many solid conclusions about just how to help people improve their thinking skills, but they do have some useful ideas. One of the most interesting is the concept of *metacognition*. This, simply put, is the process of being aware of one's own thinking process and exercising control over how that process is directed. Good thinkers seem more skilled at keeping track of their own thinking than less skilled thinkers.

Metacognition in the tech support process might mean asking yourself if you really understand what the caller's problem is, planning how to approach it, keeping track of what's been tried and failed, and being aware of important gaps in your knowledge about the situation. Being more aware of your thinking process helps you to change gears when problems don't yield to early attempts at solutions. The upshot is that support people should try to develop the knack of observing their own thinking as they tackle technical problems. This might mean asking yourself questions. "Do I really understand what the caller is saying?" "What should we try next?" "Where have I heard something like this before?" It might also mean performing a *post mortem* after a solution is finally found, asking yourself, "Why was it so hard to get to the answer? What got in the way?" Becoming a self-aware troubleshooter is one of the keys to rapid improvement.

Another interesting idea from the cognitive science folks is the concept of *heuristics*. Heuristics, simply put, are rules of thumb, informal procedures you use to solve problems. Heuristics aren't the same as algorithms, which are detailed, step-by-step instructions for carrying out a task. In order to program a computer you need an algorithm because the computer doesn't deal in anything but specifics. But when you have to solve a real-world problem, a computer glitch or whatever, you need some basic support heuristics. "If application behaves strangely, simplify configuration and test again," or "Try easy test procedures first." This chapter is intended to provide you with some basic heuristics that should be useful whatever the hardware or software you're working with. Learning to do support means mastering these general guidelines as well as the specific heuristics that apply to the individual products you're working with.

Taking Calls: The Preliminaries

As we'll see, there are several kinds of calls that come into the support center, each demanding a different type of handling. We'll deal with those different types in some detail later, but now let's look at the first steps in taking all support calls.

Answer the phone. Setting aside the details of sophisticated phone systems, which may "preanswer" calls with the name of the company and perhaps give callers a series of choices about which line to be routed to, the start of the tech support process is the moment when you, the tech, answers a ringing phone. You might have an opening script that tells the caller they've reached a help line, gives your name, and perhaps asks for the name of the caller and the product that's being called about. Obviously, it's important that the caller identify the exact product and model or version number that's the subject of the call. To the caller, such details may be unimportant but they're crucial to you.

Check entitlement. Shortly after the initial greeting, many tech support operations require that the user confirm his entitlement to help, according to standards determined by management. This often means requesting that the user supply a number which you may check against a database or printed list of authorized support recipients.

Often manufacturers' support people take serial numbers but make no effort to confirm entitlement, since registration lags behind purchase and time spent checking entitlement may not be deemed cost-effective. This may mean that some people who have unauthorized copies of a software product get help, but many companies feel they make up for that cost by keeping all calls shorter. More problematic is failing to check entitlement when there is a fee for support—it's annoying to callers who have gone to the expense of paying for support contracts only to find that no one bothers to check. This occurs because some techs just don't like the idea of fee-based support, or don't like the trouble of checking for entitlement. If your organization charges for support or gives support only to registered users, whether you like it or not, you'd best get with the program.

One class of callers to manufacturers' support lines, those who have not yet bought the product, are a special case. Most companies try to supply these people with information by way of customer service departments, separate from technical support lines, but some of the questions of presales callers may be more technical than customer service can answer. Obviously, these callers are making judgments about the suitability of the product and that includes the quality of technical support, so provision should be made to provide accurate technical information to presales callers.

Some are more entitled than others. In real-world support work, there's another aspect of entitlement that's rarely talked about. You must check whether the caller is entitled to "VIP service." In theory, we'd like to think we always give first-class service, but in reality, there's first class and then there's *first class*. If you work on a corporate help desk and get a call from the president or the president's secretary, you'll probably want to pull out all the stops to give the best service you're capable of, bending the rules, perhaps, to prioritize this problem above others. If you represent a manufacturer and get a call from a major client, you may want to treat the call with a little more urgency than normal. These are times when going the extra mile can be important to the success of the organization.

Determine what the caller needs. After the initial greetings and entitlement checking are accomplished, some phrase such as "How may I help you?" is in order. The caller finally has the floor and proceeds to explain what's happening, what information is needed, etc. Your first obligation is to try to understand *exactly* what the caller needs. This is often difficult because the caller describes the situation from his unique point of view, not yours. The caller may lack technical sophistication or may have an abundance of it, but either way, the situation described may be completely unclear after the caller's first description.

It's very common for callers to begin with an extensive inventory of their equipment configurations before getting to a statement of their problem or question. They're trying to be conscientious, assuming you want such details right from the beginning, but they don't know how hard it is to get a handle on the caller's needs without a concise statement of the problem or question. Sometimes I politely interrupt a caller's recitation with a question like, "Excuse me, but I wonder if you could give me a short description of the problem before we get to the details?" Most people don't mind the interruption. Once I have some sense of the context, the details the caller presents are often helpful. Before that, they're just confusing.

At this point, we've got a fix on what our caller needs and the way you handle the call from here on out depends on the specific type of call it is.

Types of Calls

Calls can be broken down into four main categories.

- Customer service. "I need to upgrade my copy of your software," or "Where's the nearest service center?"

- Feedback. "Your product stinks," or "Your product has saved my life," or "I'd like to request that your product be made compatible with SuperSimple Plus."

- Questions, requests for technical information. "How can I do such-and-such?" "Will you talk me through this process?" "What does the first paragraph on page 24 mean?"

- Technical problems. "I'm trying to print labels and nothing happens," or "My computer screen got completely messed up when I loaded your program."

Of course, many calls involve combinations of these types, and it may be possible to categorize a single call as a question ("Why doesn't it work?"), a problem ("I can't get it to work."), feedback ("Your product doesn't work!"), or customer service ("I want my money back!"). The point of categorization is to focus on the ways the tech support process differs according to the primary thrust of the call. You'll use different approaches for each type, even without consciously classifying them. We'll look now at the four main types of calls—customer service, feedback, questions, and problems—and suggest ways that you can handle each of them most efficiently.

Customer Service

By customer service, I mean all the nontechnical operations that help the users of your products. It includes such fundamental services as direct sales, furnishing product literature, referring callers to service centers, explaining warranties, and replacing defective products. In internal support—help desk operations—customer service, though not often called that, is still important. End-users need all sorts of assistance and information beyond purely technical matters.

The dividing line between technical support and customer service issues is often blurry but it's real and it's best defined in terms of the personnel and training requirements for the two functions. Technical support people need *technical* expertise and training as well as customer relations skills. Customer service people need great people skills and must be familiar with the technical products they deal with, but they need more training on company *policies and procedures* than on technology.

Given this distinction, and given the fact that this book is about technical support, there's still something to say about customer service. Customer service issues constantly interact with technical ones. The tech support person will often find that callers need customer service help instead of or in addition to the technical kind. What do you tell the caller to do after you've determined that his power supply is on the fritz or his disk is bad? How do you help him buy one of your company's products? Here are some key points to help you give better customer service.

Learn Company Customer Service Policies and Keep Up with Changes

Tech support folks need to know customer service policies and procedures as well as technical issues to be able to help their callers effectively. If you determine that a caller has a defective product, you want to be able to say with confidence just how the problem should be dealt with. If you're on a corporate help desk, you need to know how the company handles all the problems that come up with computers—how software is purchased, who to call if a computer needs to be moved, or who replaces toner cartridges, for example. This kind of knowledge can be just as important as knowing how to do a mail merge or structure a spreadsheet. There's one constant about policies. They're always changing. Do whatever you have to keep yourself up to date. And if you're in a position to influence the development of your organization's service policies, don't be shy about adding a tech support perspective.

Make Friends with Customer Service

Tech support and customer service share the front line position in providing customer satisfaction, so it makes sense that they should work as allies. It often comes in handy to have a friend in customer service you can call on to help with a sticky problem. Customer service people often develop considerable expertise in handling the distribution channel, service centers, and other internal and external resources. It's very helpful to tap into that kind of knowledge. It can also work both ways. Customer service people sometimes need a little technical support themselves.

Learn Your Leeway

Rules and policies are important, but they never cover everything, and they sometimes need to be stretched. Organizations with strong customer service orientations give their employees a lot of latitude in handling special cases, and back those employees up when they make their best judgments. You need to develop a good sense of how much latitude your company gives you in making decisions on handling customers' problems. You don't want to have to talk to a supervisor about every judgment call— that tends to alienate customers and supervisors—but neither do you want to go way out on a limb. Staff meetings are a good place to sound out supervisors and colleagues about how they would handle tricky customer service issues.

Taking Feedback

People's lives are affected daily by the quality and design of the products we support and if we're lucky they'll tell us about it. Tech support is in a key position when it comes to getting feedback from users, both positive and negative. It has a major role in listening to the feedback and communicating it to everyone in the organization in a position to act on it.

Studies show that most people don't complain about problems with products, they just vote with their wallets (and maybe tell a dozen people about their negative experiences). People who do complain are more likely to continue to use a product, especially

if they're satisfied by the response to their feedback. User feedback can point out what a company is doing right or wrong, with obvious importance to the bottom line. So when people do call and express dissatisfaction (or praise), we need to treat that feedback as a precious commodity and take it very seriously. Here are some points to remember about taking feedback.

Don't Be Defensive Though this point was made in the last chapter, it's important enough to repeat. Being open to feedback means avoiding a defensive posture with regard to the product or the company. You can't please everyone all the time, so accept users' criticism and suggestions in a business-like way and thank them sincerely for offering it.

Make Sure You Understand It It's just as important to clearly understand users' feedback as their technical problems and questions. Ask clarifying questions and try restating your understanding of the point they're making. Sometimes we get so focused on the way our products are designed that we have a hard time taking in users' requests for something different. Yet users often have great ideas, if we take the time to understand them.

Make Sure the Caller Understands the Issues Sometimes a caller's feedback is based on an incorrect understanding of the product. Without discounting what he has to say, it's sometimes possible to tactfully rectify his misunderstanding as revealed by his feedback. Maybe he's asking for something that's already there. Maybe he's complaining about something that he can easily change himself.

Resolve Complaints, if Possible

Negative feedback means something has gone wrong, and there's often plenty of wrong to go around. Both the user and the company may have contributed to the problem to a greater or lesser extent. If someone calls with a complaint, it's important to register it but it's more important to see if there's something you can do to resolve the problem now. Don't assume the matter is closed and the customer's problem can't be solved.

Document and Route the Feedback

It takes some time and it's not always clear what the payoff is, but it's important to record the feedback you get from callers and pass it along to the people who can use it. It's a waste when people in engineering or product development never get the word from users about what they want in future products or revisions. And remember that feedback from users comes not only in explicit complaint and praise calls but also during question and problem calls. Make sure that any useful feedback gets recorded, no matter what the context. Special feedback forms or an electronic mail system that routes the feedback to interested parties are helpful in making the feedback process work. Whatever the system, use it.

Questions, Questions, Questions

A large percentage of calls, perhaps 30 percent to 50 percent in a typical tech support operation, are from people asking for information rather than presenting technical problems, feedback, or requests for customer service. It might seem that answering questions would be a simple process. After all, you should have all the technical information about supported products in your head or at your fingertips. There shouldn't be much problem with delivering the answers. As usual, there's more to it than that, as we'll see below in looking more closely at the process of answering technical questions.

Questions and Documentation

Users call with questions when they cannot find (or have not looked for) the information they seek in user documentation. Techs often vent their frustration over callers who seem pathologically unable to open their manuals and find the information that would help them use their software or hardware efficiently. There's an off-color acronym—R.T.F.M.—that expresses this frustration.

Computer users, on the other hand, love to complain about the poor quality of documentation. It's too technical, not technical enough, written with no respect for the English (or any other) language, poorly organized, and has a lousy index to boot. Get documentation writers together and they complain that their job is nearly impossible. They're called in at the end of the development cycle, have severely limited time to write, insufficient access to engineers, and aren't paid well enough or given enough respect.

Though the documentation process seems to be maturing, chances are that computer users are going to be calling tech support lines for information for a long time to come. For one thing, there's no way that any user documentation could anticipate the infinite variety of questions that active, inquisitive users will come up with.

Sorting out Questions

Infinite though they may be, technical support questions can usually be divided into the following broad categories.

- Presales. "What are the product's features?" "What hardware and software do I need to run it?"

- Interfacing. "Is Product X compatible with Product Y?" "How do I get them talking to each other?"

- Technical. "What are the pin outs to hook your equipment to a Blahblah 390?" "Can your software be loaded into expanded memory?"

- Clarification. "What does the manual mean by 'parallel' cable?" "What does this error message mean?"

- Procedural. "How do I install it?" "How do I do such-and-such?"

Interestingly, of these five categories, it's the last one— procedural—that yields most of the could-have-found-it-in-the-manual type questions that drive tech support people crazy. Presales callers obviously don't have manuals, and marketing literature covers only limited technical information. Usually only the most common interfacing questions are covered. Tough technical questions may be unanswered by documentation, which is often aimed at the "average" user who needs only a functional description of the product and it's use. Even if the technical information is available in the documentation, the user may not have the expertise to locate or understand it.

Clarification questions are sometimes a direct reflection of problems with documentation, sometimes simply a result of the ambiguity of language and the user's unfamiliarity with computer concepts. Once again, we have to remember that not everyone lives and breaths computers, and even if they do, there's always plenty of room for confusion. User questions provide valuable feedback. If one person finds the manual unclear and calls for clarification, many more probably were equally confused but remained silent.

Procedural questions range from callers simply wanting to be walked through the installation process because they're intimidated by technical manuals, to people asking for help with complex application development. Some would say that neither of these types of requests should be satisfied by tech support, that they constitute basic computer training on the one hand and consulting on the other.

These are basic policy questions that should be decided, at least in broad terms, by management. Certainly, they shouldn't be decided on an ad hoc basis by a tech support person based on his mood, stress level, or response to the caller's personality. Nonetheless, you always have some discretion in judging what approach to take with a particular caller.

Dealing with Nonreaders

Like most support people I sometimes get miffed with folks who want to avoid any contact with the manual, who want me to explain every procedure to them. Maybe it's puritanical, but even though I enjoy helping people who have tried to help themselves, I feel frustrated repeating explanations I know any literate person could follow if he tried reading the manual. I believe there are sound reasons for avoiding unnecessary "walk throughs." Procedural explanations like this can be extremely time-consuming, and I doubt they aid learning for most people. On the other hand, it's good to remember that not everyone learns in the same way. Some seem to do better with oral explanations than written ones. And whether they're a little lazy or not, these folks are our customers, the ones who ultimately write our checks!

I usually try to tactfully direct the caller toward the place in the manual where the topic is covered, pointing out any common pitfalls or problems. Then I ask whether he'd like to try the procedure on his own and call back if he needs help, or have me go through it with him step by step. Most people need just a little encouragement and direction to dig into the manuals and gain the confidence that comes from solving problems themselves. If a caller prefers I don't hesitate to take the step-by-step approach.

Some Questions Shouldn't Be Answered

Questions can be categorized in many ways (smart/stupid, easy/hard, etc.), but one of the most important distinctions for manufacturer's tech support is between questions that should be answered and questions that shouldn't. Most tech support people seem to have an instinctive desire to answer any question to which they know the answer, and it may be unnatural to think of refusing to answer some questions. However, organizations have a right to control the information they make available about their products and operations. There are sound business reasons to refuse to answer some questions. If a caller asks about a future product release—what features it will have and when it will be available, for example—it is perfectly legitimate to politely refuse to supply the information. Such information is proprietary, subject to change, and could benefit a competitor. It's up to the company to decide when to reveal it. Sometimes people even call to ask about the economic condition of the company or other business details that have nothing to do with technical matters.

Just what information should be revealed by tech support staff is a decision for management to make and communicate to the people on the phones. It's hard to lay out blanket policies that anticipate every sensitive area that you are privy to. You need guidelines but also some sensitivity to company security issues. Think carefully before providing information that could be sensitive. "When in doubt, check it out!"

Setting Limits
Besides proprietary information, manufacturer support operations have to make decisions about answering questions that go beyond the basic operation of their own products. Some callers ask about very technical details of programming or design. Others ask about products made by other manufacturers that are used in conjunction with the support organization's product. Then there are the requests for step-by-step help in building a complex application. The latter is closer to computer consulting than technical support, and as such may be beyond the support a company feels it should offer. Judgments must also be made when the caller's questions reflect technical curiosity rather than functional need, especially if considerable research is needed to answer them.

The support person needs guidelines to make these kinds of decisions, though there will always be a need for judgment and flexibility. Some companies are liberal on these matters, attempting to answer almost every question that comes their way to the best of their ability. Others are conservative in setting limits to the subjects they will answer questions about. The liberal approach may make more callers happy initially, but it means longer calls as well as support people being tempted to answer questions that go beyond their training. As with most things, the art is to find the right balance.

One class of callers, the extremely novice computer user, presents special problems to any tech support operation. Explaining a complex installation procedure to someone with little or no experience with computers can be a frustrating, time-consuming process. The interpersonal aspects of working with such callers are discussed in Chapter 3, *Communication Skills,* but a word here is in order. The question of how much training of novice users you should do is another management decision and that decision should be based on such issues as the complexity of the product, the market for which it was developed, and the price. If there's a policy that some level of computer familiarity is required before a user is qualified for tech support, that policy should be stated clearly in the user documentation, and the policy should be implemented tactfully by tech support.

In other tech support contexts, such as in a corporate help desk, there may be more of a blending of training and help line functions. Support personnel may have a clear responsibility to answer every request for "hand holding," whether or not the user has done his homework. However, it may be better to get completely inexperienced callers into computer training programs than repeatedly leading them step by step through basic procedures.

Question-answering Basics

Questions don't usually cause you the kind of difficulties that troubleshooting (discussed below) can, but there is still some skill required to answer them effectively. Let's look at some key points.

Understand. It seems obvious but it's not always easy. Understanding the caller's question means understanding the context in which it's asked. I've found that I don't really understand a question until I understand why a caller wants to know the answer, how the question fits into the caller's use of the product I'm supporting. People are usually more than happy to explain. Sometimes you find that the literal question being asked is far from what the questioner really needs to know. It's important to ask enough clarifying questions to understand the caller's needs. This is especially true when dealing with novices.

Think. The next step is to consult your own memory for the answer. Many questions are perennials, asked over and over by new users, or users with common interfacing and compatibility issues. It's handy to be able to answer common questions from the top of your head, but be careful about confirming answers with other sources if you have any doubts about the details.

Search. There are always new questions, of course, and the answers are not always at hand. The most important skill for people who answer questions is the ability to choose where to look for information, to think in terms of where it is likely to be recorded or who is likely to have it in his head. This means learning to use tables of contents and indexes in documentation (even crummy ones), learning to jockey sophisticated online knowledgebases, as well as becoming attuned to your colleagues' areas of expertise.

If there's a chance to get the answer by putting someone on hold and asking colleagues or supervisors for the information, it's often more efficient than ending the call, doing the research and calling back. The ability to make the judgment about which route to take comes with experience. You may disturb someone else's work flow by interrupting them in your search for an answer, but you will surely save time and energy if you don't have to go through the process of calling someone back. Well-run organizations have formal and informal procedures to deal with these situations.

Write. The answers to frequently asked questions should be added to the next version of the documentation. Answers to any significant question should be recorded in the support center's knowledgebase. It's a small tragedy when a question has to be researched more than once.

Troubleshooting

Troubleshooting is what most people think of when they think of technical support. It's both the most difficult and the most rewarding part of the job. To triumph over a really tricky technical problem over the phone can make you feel like Sherlock Holmes, Mr. Wizard, and Sigmund Freud all at once. Well, almost.

Some people seem to have a knack for sorting out complex tangles quickly. Others tend to founder whenever they encounter new, uncharted problems. What are the skills possessed by ace troubleshooters? Can they be taught? Is experience the only teacher?

You *do* have to do a fair amount of troubleshooting before you get good at it. I believe you can learn faster by studying the process step by step, noting the approaches that mark the skillful troubleshooter. There are no short cuts, no simple tricks to becoming an expert, but there are some techniques anyone can learn to improve efficiency.

Problems Need Solutions

Troubleshooting is really a two-part process. The first part is *problem determination*, which simply means finding the cause of the problem symptoms your caller is reporting. The second part is *problem resolution*, which obviously means supplying the caller with a solution to his problem. We're going to concentrate on the problem determination part of the equation since that's the part that causes the most headaches and requires the most adjustment to our normal ways of thinking. Problem resolution is also critical and it's worth some discussion here at the outset. Here are some common resolutions for the kinds of problems that come into support centers.

- Explain user error.

- Recommend a product that solves problem.

- Refer caller to manufacturer of faulty product.

- Ship patch or other product modification to solve problem.

- Find and offer workaround for faulty feature.

- Refer problem to engineering for correction of bug or faulty design.

- Refer caller to hardware service facility.

- Explain minor repair or patch procedure.

- Explain to caller that there is no solution, and why.

Many of these solutions require the cooperation of people outside of the support organization, from your own company's engineering staff to independent service centers, to other companies' support centers. Support departments vary widely as to how much research and engineering they do. Generally, when it comes to product modification, bug fixes, and hardware servicing, support centers function as referral, coordination, and delivery agents rather than as the ultimate service providers. Maintaining close and cooperative relationships with the other folks that we rely on is vital to the success of the support center and the organization as a whole.

One of the most important things that support can do is develop consistent, efficient solutions to the common problems that callers report. A guiding principle should be that whenever a problem is reported, it is almost certain that more than one user will experience it. Therefore, it's important to keep track of solutions and to rationalize their dissemination. Think of the common case of a software patch for a known bug. If a support person has to painstakingly search through dozens of files, copy the patch onto a disk, put the disk in a mailer, then address, stamp, and mail the package each time the patch is needed by a caller, a lot of time will be wasted. Time put into organizing and automating the process will pay big dividends.

Problem Determination Principles

Back to the fun part—tracking down the causes of tricky problems. Before we get to the step-by-step description of problem determination, let's look at some general principles to guide the process.

Strive for efficiency. Though there's no universal troubleshooting strategy, it's clear that you want to avoid a random, unsystematic search for problem causes—exploring one possibility inconclusively, skipping to something else (with no particular reason in mind), losing track of what's been checked, gathering random, unfocused information. Most troubleshooters probably fall into such patterns sometimes, even the most experienced ones, usually when faced with nasty, unyielding problems that seem to defy all attempts at logic. Remember though that skilled troubleshooters use search strategies that are as disciplined and logical as possible. You can always pause and rethink your strategy in the middle of a call, even if you started out haphazardly.

Plan what you can. Troubleshooting is full of surprises, but still it's more efficient if you can do a little planning before diving into the maelstrom. Try to mentally sketch out a plan of attack to guide the search process. Something like, "Hmmm, first we should check for A, then if that doesn't work, we'll look at B. C is a strong possibility, but let's hold off on that because it's harder to test for."

Though you might assume that it's always better to check the likeliest causes of a problem first, it's often more efficient to look first at things that are most easily tested, even if they're not the most likely problem causes. This means you'll have to assess the difficulty of different tests, estimate how likely it is the tests will yield solutions, and factor these judgments together in developing your game plan. This kind of thinking gets much easier with experience, but putting a little thought into planning will help even beginners.

Don't let the clock beat you. In most support jobs there's pressure to keep calls as short as possible. The cost of "talk time" is high, and so, usually, is the number of people calling for help. You may be told that your performance is judged partially by how long your call average is. This can lead to a lot of stress when you're faced with a tough call that seems to take forever. The time pressure can make it harder to think and communicate clearly, which makes the solution take even longer. Try to remember that it's *average* call length that counts, and that long calls are normal. There will be some short calls to balance them out. On the other hand, don't go on forever troubleshooting a problem if there's little likelihood of coming to a solution. You're better off trying to research the problem offline, or escalating it to others who are designated as your back-up.

Engage your visual sense. Telephone troubleshooting is tough because you have to make sense of the caller's words, which are often inaccurate, then translate the content into the kinds of images most of us need for efficient problem-solving. You have to keep all this information in your head as you verbally interact with your caller. I find the most valuable troubleshooting tools are paper and a pencil. I use them to draw diagrams of complicated systems, create a matrix showing test results under different conditions, and doodle while waiting for the caller to complete an operation. Grid paper makes the whole thing seem more scientific. The important thing, however, is to engage the mind's eye in solving problems and to relieve the brain from having to keep track of everything. So far as I know, no tech support software has yet come along that can beat a scratch pad for this kind of thing.

Go the extra mile. Many times a troubleshooting call offers an opportunity to do a little extra for the caller. This might mean offering a useful productivity tip or heading off a future problem you can anticipate from what the caller has told you. Even though you have an interest in keeping calls brief, this extra effort can often mean more satisfied customers for your organization, and even head off future calls.

Troubleshooting One Step at a Time

Now let's trace the typical troubleshooting session step by step. I'll use a number of examples from my experience supporting printers and printing utilities, but the principles are the same whatever the product. Not all steps are required for every call, and sometimes the order is different, but the troubleshooting process usually follows the path below.

Step 1: Listen to the problem. Your first job is to understand the problem, though the caller's first description may not be much help. Some people spill out a flood of details about their systems, what went wrong, what happened Tuesday, why it couldn't possibly be their fault, and so on. Others give a terse "It doesn't work" kind of report. Neither approach is what you need to solve the problem.

The kind of trouble report you need is of a very specific form. "When I try to do X, Y happens." Let's call this the problem statement. The caller often just presents the "Y happens" part of the statement, but you need to be just as clear about exactly what the caller is trying to accomplish. Without that, there's no way to tell whether the symptom is normal system behavior (and user misunderstanding) or a "real" problem. You listen carefully to the caller's report so that you can repeat back to the caller your understanding of the problem statement. "Okay, so what's happening is that when you try to do X, Y happens. Is that right?" The caller can then correct the statement, clarify the problem, or agree to your restatement. If you neglect to offer a restatement of the problem you risk wasting time trying to solve the wrong problem, which is Cardinal Sin #1 in the troubleshooting business.

From the beginning, it's important to remember that many callers' perspective on their problems is shaped by their desire to accomplish a task and frustration that it's not working properly. Right or wrong, they're often suspicious (or sure) that the problem is caused by a faulty product. Many users have little understanding of exactly what the product is designed to do and what kinds of system behavior are normal. The product may appear "broken" or to have a bug because it's not doing what they want. And there is always a chance that there *is* some bug in the system (or a hardware malfunction). Although very few calls actually end up revealing bugs, you have to keep an open mind about the possibility.

When you discover that the caller is trying to do something that the product isn't designed for, you'll want to clarify the specifications of the product at this point. You don't want to imply that the caller's desired feature or capability is "off the wall." In fact, you should treat it as a valuable suggestion for future development. If the caller has received an incorrect impression about what the product should be expected to do, it's helpful to find out where it came from. Was training incomplete? Were marketing claims exaggerated? Did a dealer make too strong a pitch? Is advertising or documentation unclear? You may be able to prevent future misunderstandings by conveying this information to responsible parties within your organization.

Step 2: Search your memory. This is pretty obvious. As soon as you have a problem statement you're confident of you listen for bells going off in your head. "This sounds like something I've heard before." Depending on your experience and training, you've probably got a powerful internal knowledgebase of previously encountered problems. This is probably too early in the troubleshooting process to undertake a search of online knowledgebases or special support documentation, but not too soon to consult your own memory in an attempt to bring the call to a speedy and successful conclusion.

Usually, a limited number of problems occurs again and again. They may be bugs or they may be common user errors or misunderstandings. Initial training should have covered some of these recurring problems and experience adds to the list. When you suspect the caller is reporting a recurrent problem, zero in, asking questions to confirm whether this is indeed another example of the familiar problem. You can then offer the stock solution, if there is one. The successful implementation of the solution provides the ultimate test that your quick diagnosis was correct. When you're able to cut off the troubleshooting session early by quickly recognizing one of the usual suspects, everybody wins.

Step 3: Ask clarifying questions. Assuming the problem doesn't quickly reveal itself as a classic, it's time to dig for more information. You ask a series of questions to clarify what the caller is trying to do, how they're doing it, and how the system is responding. During this clarification process, it's important to ask very concrete questions.

"Where exactly is the first line printing?"

"What colors are appearing on your screen?"

"Read me the error message word for word."

"Does the problem occur every time you try to do it?"

You begin the troubleshooting process with little sense of how accurate the caller's perceptions of symptoms might be or how well he or she might have followed the proper procedures. Asking concrete questions leads to a better understanding of where the problem lies rather than taking the initial reports for granted. As any detective would tell you, most people are not keen observers. Asking detailed questions can lead to much better information. Some generic questions are frequently useful.

"Have you made any changes in your system?"

"Has the process worked in the past?"

"Was the system moved recently?"

"Was some new software installed?"

You're trying to pinpoint the cause of the problem by asking about any changes in the system. Events the user considers very minor can tip you off to a problem cause.

Step 4: Try quick fixes. Experienced troubleshooters usually have some handy quick fixes to try before they really get their hands dirty on a problem. Things like checking the printer cable, powering down and up the computer, or reinstalling the software don't cost too much in terms of telephone time or user aggravation. They've been proven effective many times before. There may be no logical reason to suspect that the cable is loose, but if the printer is acting weirdly, it's probably worth a try.

Like any kind of skilled worker, a troubleshooter strives for economy. The most result for the least effort. Troubleshooters aren't lazy, but they know that the process of tracking down a problem when they have no good clue about where it lies can take a long time.

If there are some quick things that prove effective a reasonable percentage of the time, it's worth a try to cut short the problem-solving process. Learning the useful quick fixes in a specific domain might come through listening to an expert troubleshooter or perhaps as part of an organization's initial training program. Your bag of tricks will get bigger through experience.

Step 5: Check for user error. Many problems are caused by users' mistakes and misunderstandings. To determine if the caller is operating the system correctly you ask early in the call what he is doing step by step. You need to know the procedure by heart or follow the documentation carefully to confirm that the caller is doing it right.

Often callers won't be able to tell you exactly what they've been doing—they just don't remember the details. Others might hesitate to tell you because they're afraid you'll point out their mistakes. Nobody likes to appear foolish. To avoid putting the caller on the spot, you can say something like, "Let's go over the steps in the manual." Then ask tactfully if each step was carried out as described. Even better is having the caller carry out the procedure while you follow along in the manual or do the same procedure on your system (see Step 7 below). That's why it's best when users place support calls from the problem site so that they can reproduce the problem and try solutions while you're still on the line.

If you discover user error, you obviously need to explain where the caller went wrong, which may simply mean referring to a page in the manual or "hand holding" the user through the process on the phone. The key word in this process is tact. It doesn't hurt to say something like, "the manual could be a little clearer on that." Chances are, it could.

If the caller seems to be doing everything right, it's time to look at other possible causes. Nevertheless, experienced trouble-shooters know that the possibility of user error isn't completely eliminated until some other cause is found for the problem. We can never be quite certain that the caller is reporting correctly exactly what he is doing. If the troubleshooting process proves difficult it may be useful to come back again to the issue of user error, especially if one begins to get a sense that the caller can't be considered completely reliable.

Step 6: Check the configuration. Does the caller's system meet the requirements of the supported product? Product documentation should state what basic configuration is required, but it won't go into detail about all the possible variations and compatibility problems. And, unfortunately, many callers don't know much about what's inside their systems. Your knowledge of the products you support will usually tell you which aspects of the system configuration are relevant to the problem you're dealing with, so you can focus your questions there. There are times when you have to ask the caller to find someone else onsite who can answer your configuration questions.

At this early stage in the troubleshooting process, you'll normally do only a general survey of the caller's system configuration to see that it meets basic requirements. If further diagnostic efforts hit a brick wall you might have to come back to this step again. Only then it will probably mean going into considerably more depth.

Step 7: Get back to vanilla. Experience shows that a large number of software and hardware glitches are caused by compatibility problems between various products. Despite the fact that microcomputer architecture is supposed to be "open" and capable of infinite reconfiguration, and that software is supposed to be "well behaved," manufacturers know that their products can't possibly work properly with everything else and sometimes get into mutual blaming matches about who's not playing by the rules.

The upshot is that one of the most likely culprits when the product you support doesn't work right is some other product. The way to check for these conflicts is to eliminate as many variables as possible, to get the caller's system as close as possible to a "plain vanilla" configuration. Eliminate concurrently operating software, take special interface devices (such as networks or switch boxes) out of the picture, and try to have the caller reduce his system to the most generic, "vanilla" configuration he can. If simplifying the system solves the problem, try adding other products one by one until you can pinpoint exactly where the conflict lies.

Sometimes a simpler alternative to complete "vanillization" is to eliminate parts of the system one by one to see if problems go away. Your first step when trying to diagnose software problems on an MS-DOS computer, for example, might be to have the user boot from a floppy disk instead of the hard disk. This eliminates the effects of memory resident software, AUTOEXEC.BAT, CONFIG.SYS files, and hard disk problems in one relatively simple step. In hardware troubleshooting, instead of simply eliminating parts of the system, you often have to substitute known good components for ones you're testing. For example, swap a good I/O board for one that might be causing a problem. Make sure though that you're substituting a good part and not another lemon.

Finding simple ways for users to eliminate possible conflicts makes your life a lot easier. Unlike troubleshooting in the field, you have to depend on your caller to carry out diagnostic procedures correctly. There are times when your judgment will tell you that a particular caller can't be relied upon to do any system reconfiguration at all, or only a limited amount. You might then have to try to get the caller to enlist more knowledgeable onsite help.

Step 8: Try it yourself. At this point you've determined that the caller is attempting something the product is supposed to do, he seems to be doing it right, and he has the required system configuration. Now it's time to try to carry out the procedure on your system to make sure that the process works as it should. Of course, this might not be necessary if it's something you've done a dozen times. It might not be possible if the caller's problem arises only under very specific circumstances that you can't duplicate. You may not be able to duplicate an unusual hardware configuration or software environment, in which case you'll have to skip this step. In most cases, though, you should be able to confirm whether the process works under normal conditions on your system or other testing setup in your department. There are two possible outcomes when you test the procedure on your system: it fails, or it succeeds. Let's talk about failure first.

Welcome to bugland. Supposing your tests duplicate the caller's problem. Then you've probably discovered a bug and if it hasn't been documented before you should consider yourself lucky to have found it. Of course, the caller actually discovered the bug, but you should take some credit for putting it on the map. Some bugs are minor, some fatal. Some show up under very specific conditions, and these are the ones that are likely to get past the product testing process and only get discovered when a user exercises the product in the field. Manufacturers maintain lists of known bugs, of course. If you work for the manufacturer of the product you're supporting, you'll want to consult the bug list and see if your bug has been spotted before. If you're doing internal support you'll probably have to contact the manufacturer to check for known bugs and report the one you've found. Getting some companies to admit to a bug is like extracting a confession, but the better ones will admit to problems and work on them.

What the caller needs when he's got a bug is either a fix or a workaround. Tech support is likely to be more involved in disseminating these than in developing them, but that varies with the product, the problem, and the organization. If you don't have a solution you'll have to get back to the caller later. Try to gauge the urgency of the problem for the caller and document the bug thoroughly. Submit a bug report to the folks who handle such things. Take a professional interest in the resolution of the problem. Do what you have to do to make sure that the caller who discovered the bug gets a solution or workaround as soon as one is available.

If, however, the test succeeds, you'll have to keep on searching. If you are able to succeed with the procedure on your system but your caller can't, you're going to have to dig deeper. Somehow the caller's system differs from yours and it's not obvious how. The order in which you apply the next four steps will depend on your assessment of the kind of problem you're dealing with and the resources you have available.

Step 9: Check the knowledgebase. Your support center no doubt keeps tons of valuable, up-to-date documentation, all perfectly organized, and instantly available at your fingertips. No? Well, there's bound to be *some* information resource to aid support, and this may be the time to consult it. The questions to ask yourself are is the solution to your problem likely to be in the knowledgebase somewhere, and how are you going to find it?

Chapter 5, *Information Techniques and Tools,* contains an extensive discussion of information resources for support and how to organize and use them, so I won't go into detail here. One key point though—your ability to find information in a knowledgebase or printed documentation usually depends on being able to name the problem (or key factors in the problem) in the same way the information is designated in the knowledgebase. That's why it's usually easier to find information about compatibility issues with specific products (Lotus 1-2-3, H-P LaserJet printer, etc.) than about more abstract problems ("squiggly lines on screen," "failure to print pound sign"). Lots of progress is being made in finding better ways to organize and access technical information, but your success with a knowledge-base will still depend on your familiarity with its organization, comprehensiveness, and style.

Step 10: Use troubleshooting aids and diagnostics. If you're lucky, you'll have access to some troubleshooting tools in addition to a knowledgebase, and now is probably the time to use them. I'm talking about such things as question scripts, diagnostic charts, schematics, and expert systems. These tools provide logical guidance in searching for the cause of problems.

In electronic equipment troubleshooting there are schematic diagrams which indicate proper voltage or other values at various points in a circuit. The troubleshooting procedure in the field is to check the values until it becomes clear that one is not correct. Individual components can thus be sequentially eliminated as possible culprits.

In telephone technical support such direct testing procedures are generally not available, but there are still plenty of trouble-shooting aids that can be valuable. One of the simplest is a series of questions, the series being structured into a logical sequence, and each of the questions having been designed to elicit essential information. These key questions are asked of any caller whose problem doesn't have an obvious solution.

"What version of the operating system are you using?"

"Are you using any memory resident software?"

"Are you using a network or printer sharing device?"

"Are you printing from a serial or parallel port?"

Depending on the product, the list of questions can be either simple or complex. Some of the most productive offline work you can do is to develop and polish such batteries of diagnostic questions. The payoff comes in more effective training and shorter, more uniform and efficient support calls.

More elaborate than a question script is the classic troubleshooting diagram that logically lays out the sequence of factors to check leading to a positive diagnosis. Troubleshooting a problem area using one of these diagrams should be a pretty straightforward process. You ask the caller to carry out a series of tests and report the results. You follow the diagram path suggested by the results until the diagram leads to a diagnosis of the problem and a solution.

A logical diagram like this can be on paper or embodied in a computerized expert system. An expert system automates the process of presenting salient questions to the user and using the answers to arrive at a solution. The problem is that creating such a logical schema comprehensive enough to solve real problems is difficult and time-consuming. The experience required to construct the diagram has to come from dealing with scores or hundreds of problems in the first place. Naturally, with every significant change in the product design, the troubleshooting diagrams or expert systems have to be updated or rewritten. With large, complex products it's hard to even imagine a diagram or expert system to help locate and solve most problems. The best one might hope for would be a series of diagrams or expert systems that help solve problems with subparts of the system. These can be extremely valuable if the subparts lend themselves to systematic, logical troubleshooting procedures.

Another type of troubleshooting aid is the diagnostic test or procedure that reveals facts about the condition of the system. These can be either built into the product or applied later. A nice example of a built-in diagnostic is the hex dump feature of many computer printers which allows a user to print out all the data that gets to the printer in hexadecimal characters. With a hex dump, it's possible to determine what printer commands and data are being sent to the printer and thus determine if the software printer driver is to blame for a printing error or the printer is.

Expert troubleshooters know and use the built-in diagnostics of their systems and always have a number of simple tests they can apply to help track down the source of problems. In a sense, though, you're constantly inventing new diagnostics. Each question you ask represents a test designed to reveal something new about the system. Diagnostics and questions are chosen to eliminate or confirm one thing after another as possible sources of the problem. The trick is to select the questions and diagnostics that reveal the most salient information about the system and then to take that information into account in formulating new tests, until enough information is in place to start developing some theories about what's going on. "It could either be A or B that's causing the trouble." Then more tests are formulated and applied to test the theories.

Step 11: Dissect the system. You've got a tough problem on your hands and solving it is going to take more than standard procedures. Just as in medical diagnosis, the first step is to figure out what part of the system is acting up. Your training has taught you the basic anatomy of the product, the way the subparts of the product are supposed to function, and how the product interacts with other components of the computer system. Does the nature of the problem suggest which subpart of the system is misbehaving? Are there any tests that can eliminate certain parts of the whole computer system as being responsible?

There's a classic troubleshooting technique used when you don't have a clue about where the problem lies. It's called the split half search, and I first saw it described in a little book called *Troubleshooting: The Troubleshooting Course* by Robert F. Mager (Lake Publishing Company, 1982). The idea is that when you don't know where in the system the cause might be lurking, you have to check the whole system, part by part. But the most efficient way to do this is to *conceptually* split the system into halves and eliminate one of the halves as the culprit. Then the remaining half of the system is split again, and so on. Eventually, this process should lead to the cause of the problem, and though it might take longer than if you had some clue to help zero in on the cause, it will be much more efficient than going through the system element by element. You might ask just how you can split something like a computer system into halves. Sometimes it's easy. Problem—the printer isn't printing. Is the problem with the computer hardware, software, cable, or printer? It's easy to see how you can split the system— computer&software/cable&printer.

Test to eliminate one half or the other. For example, by hooking the printer and cable to another computer and seeing if it works. Then split the remaining half of the system—computer/software.

If the test shows that the computer can print using other software, then you can conclude the problem is with the software. Next you'd troubleshoot that.

This is a fairly trivial example, but it shows a kind of thinking that can improve your troubleshooting of tough problems.

The important thing is not to split the system into perfectly equal halves, whatever that would mean, but to systematically break it down into the roughly equal segments.

Step 12: When all else fails, get help! Everyone needs help sometimes, even the experts. Using the techniques outlined here along with your knowledge of the products you support should help get to the bottom of most callers' problems, but sometimes nothing seems to work. The best technician in the world strikes out sometimes, which should make the rest of us feel better.

Sometimes difficult problems yield as soon as you find another person to describe the symptoms to. Discussing the problem, getting a fresh perspective, or just getting your ear off the phone can bring light to a tough problem. Informal communication should be encouraged. That's why support facilities should have open layouts with few walls, to aid communication. If you're stuck on a problem, you might ask your caller if you may put them on hold so you can consult with a colleague.

Sometimes you have to give up. You can't solve them all. Every support organization needs escalation procedures to pass the real stumpers along to individuals or teams with the expertise and the time to research, test, and solve them. Or you might be able to solve the problem yourself, given a little time to discuss it and experiment.

Whenever you can't solve a problem immediately, your first concern is to document the call and make sure it doesn't "drop through the cracks." Make a commitment to get an answer or progress report to your caller at an appropriate time and keep it!

Let's Get Real! Real problems are tough—if they weren't they'd hardly be worth talking about. Troubleshooting in the real world sometimes means having hunches, getting lost, backtracking ("Wait, I thought we eliminated that!"), and sometimes logic doesn't seem to play much role in it. I've tried to collect some of the recurring situations that cause tech support people grief. Though they can't be eliminated, a little awareness may make it easier to disarm these demons.

Beware the red herring! Sometimes there's an obvious cause for a problem but it's not the real cause. If a caller informs you he's sure the hardware is malfunctioning because yesterday's storm sent a surge through the power lines, take the idea into consideration. But if you focus exclusively on the storm-damage theory without eliminating more likely causes—such as user error or a loose cable—you might get bitten by the dreaded red herring. A red herring is really just some potential cause that draws all your attention while the real cause hides elsewhere. What you can do to prevent wasting time is to avoid focusing on one possible cause to the exclusion of all the others. If a caller is sure the problem is caused by such and such, just say to yourself, "Maybe."

"Yesterday it was working, today it's not, and we didn't change anything, honest!" Software doesn't break, so it's amazing how often callers complain that their software doesn't work suddenly for no apparent reason. Hardware does break, but not usually without some warning. When someone complains of a sudden change in system performance without any action on his part it is often productive to ask him to think back very carefully about any changes that may have been made to his system, no matter how seemingly insignificant. Ask if a colleague could have changed the configuration, or if the system has been moved. Check cabling for inadvertent disconnection.

"First I had this problem, then that happened, and then..." Sometimes callers have such a tangled mess of problems that you hardly know where to start. They may be so confused that they infect you with hopelessness about ever getting to the root or roots of the difficulty. You've got to slow these people (and yourself) down and deal with each symptom at a pace you can handle. Use a paper and pencil to list the key factors and sketch the situation schematically if possible.

"Oh, I forgot to mention..." Callers often neglect to mention vital facts about their systems unless you ask them directly. I've been well along the troubleshooting path trying to diagnose a software problem before a caller mentioned they were working in a network environment, a fact that changes the diagnostic picture considerably. Now I know to ask early on, "Are you using a network, switch box, or other special configuration?" Don't assume you're dealing with a "normal" configuration until you've confirmed it.

"It only happened once but I want to know why!" One of the most difficult troubleshooting problems is to solve a problem that happened once and can't be repeated. Sometimes callers are convinced that some strange system behavior that happened once is vitally important and they want an answer to why it happened. If you've got a good guess about what was going on by all means give it. If not, how much time and energy should you put into troubleshooting this one-shot problem? Most people will accept the explanation that you just can't get anywhere with an unreproducible problem. It helps to ask a few questions first to eliminate common problems.

And the toughest one of all... Sometimes folks just don't tell you the truth about what they've done or what their systems are doing. They're probably not malicious—just confused, perhaps, or defensive about something. Maybe they're just not good at describing what they see. But how can you help them if they don't tell you the facts? You learn to spot this phenomenon a little better through experience. Sometimes you have to tactfully ask people to read you exactly what's on the screen. If you have a doubt about whether the caller's telling you the truth, give them the third degree, but gently!

Helping Smarter

Doing telephone technical support presents unique intellectual challenges. It calls for knowledge, ingenuity, and imagination, not to mention the human relations skills we've discussed in Chapter 3, *Communication Skills*. You've got to know the products you support backwards and forwards and you've got to solve problems, answer questions, and take feedback—with as much efficiency and patience as possible. When you pick up the phone you never know what you'll get, a simple question, a tough troubleshooting problem, or an earful of criticism. You depend on callers for the facts that help you solve their problems, but you can never take the accuracy of their descriptions for granted. It's challenging work, but there are tricks and habits that make things easier, some of which we've looked at here.

Information Techniques and Tools

The essential product of any tech support operation is information. Callers in trouble must be given the information they need to solve their problems and get on with their work. Callers with questions need answers. Training can't impart all the information support people will need to do their jobs well. Clear, concise and up-to-date information about the products being supported must be in their hands (or at their fingertips).

Though it takes time and organizational resources to develop and maintain specialized tech support information tools, they pay for themselves by shortening calls, improving accuracy, and even preventing burnout. There's nothing more frustrating than knowing a question has been answered before, but not knowing how to find the key information while the caller is on the phone. No tech support person can remember all the key facts about the products he supports, and even if one person could, that knowledge would be useless to the rest of the organization.

Quality information tools can pay other dividends. They serve as the basis for training manuals and provide crucial feedback to software designers and documentation writers. They are the source of statistics about support center productivity and individual employee performance. And they have an important if subtle role to play in legitimizing, systematizing, and rationalizing the tech support role in an organization.

The Information Menu

A successful information program should include the following elements.

- A call-tracking database to document each call received

- Annotated versions of all user documentation

- Specialized technical documentation used by inhouse programmers, engineers, and technicians

- A knowledgebase (online or on paper) containing the kind of information the technician routinely needs to answer questions not directly covered by the user manual

- An alert system to announce important changes, discoveries, and other "hot" information that everyone needs to know

- A library of software, documentation, and technical literature covering the computer environment your supported products operate in

This list makes sense for most tech support organizations, but there is hardly a universal standard in the kinds of information systems maintained by different companies. Many keep no call records at all. Though one might assume that these are the companies with terrible reputations for support, this is not necessarily so. One very highly reputed publisher (with a great support reputation) does not maintain logs of individual calls unless the calls are unresolved. But for the majority of tech support operations, call tracking, like the other systems listed above, is vital. After all, it's very hard to manage what you can't measure.

On Paper or Online? Each document type listed above, except the last, could be a paper document or an online information system. We'll discuss specific online systems in more detail later on. Many major tech support operations still maintain their information systems on paper instead of online. My own experience has shown that tech support information should be kept in both paper and electronic forms (except for call tracking, which calls out for computerization).

Paper documentation has some advantages. It can often be searched quicker and everyone is familiar with how to use it. It's easier on the eyes and can be marked, copied, and distributed easily. Paper documentation is still available when a computer is down, or when it is being used to diagnose a problem. Online systems, though, offer quicker and cheaper dissemination, very fast searching for any key word or phrase, and other valuable features, like hypertext and expert system capabilities, which we'll discuss later.

What Kind of System?

We'll discuss each of the documentation types separately, but bear in mind that they could be integrated into one networked, online information system or kept as separate systems. Developing a custom system inhouse is also an option, with fairly obvious advantages and disadvantages. No predesigned system is likely to fit the exact needs and preferences of a specific organization, but building a custom system from scratch is a major undertaking filled with unpredictable obstacles. We'll look at some of the factors involved in creating an inhouse solution below in "An Evolving Information Management System." Reading the descriptions of some of the commercially available software systems at the end of this chapter will also clarify some of the issues.

Bear in mind that multiple tech support operators require multiple workstations. In a microcomputer environment this means a networked system is probably necessary. All operators need to be able to access the database (though not necessarily the same record) simultaneously. The network system you choose has to be expandable to accommodate the maximum number of operators you can reasonably foresee needing in the future. In some companies, access to the tech support information system will be available to all employees, not just tech support staff. Network systems also require network-compatible software. Obviously, many of the benefits of networked workstations are present in mainframe terminals serving multiple terminals, but if the products supported run on PCs, each support person would probably need a PC as well as a terminal.

Whose Job Is Information?

Given the importance of quality information tools to tech support, and the resources required to develop them, an obvious question is, who will do the work? Are the tech support staff supposed to update the knowledgebase between calls? Is this a clerical function? The answer obviously depends on many factors, with economic ones at the top of the list. My own background as a librarian makes me prejudiced toward hiring professional information specialists for this function, but a technical writer with organizational skills would be another good choice, as might an experienced tech support person. Whoever the person chosen, I believe that there should be someone on staff whose job is developing and maintaining the organization's information systems. High quality information pays for itself.

Let's look at the parts of the overall information system in more detail.

Call-tracking Database

A call-tracking database can be a powerful tool for improving technical support. It allows recording such information as the name of the caller, his phone number, the product being asked about (and the version or release number), a serial number, information about the caller's hardware and any software being used, the problem being reported (or question being asked), background information elicited by the tech support person, and the answer or solution.

The system could also optionally contain fields for the caller's address (in case upgrades or patches must be sent) and a classification field where the tech support people put a code that classifies the type of call for later analysis, marking it as an installation question, for example. Since some callers will call more than once, the system should allow as much room as necessary for recording transactions. The system should mark each call with a beginning and ending time, and calculate the call length. Of course, it should also show who took the call and whether the call is completed or "closed" (answered satisfactorily). If the call is not closed, the system should produce a paper or electronic version of the call record that can be sent along to the next stage of the support process, and should be able to report all "open" calls at any time.

A Few Extras

The call-tracking database can make life easier by including some extras. An autodial feature can greatly ease callbacks by reading a caller's phone number off the screen and speed dialing it. The system could also read the caller's area code and show the appropriate time zone or even the local time in the caller's area. If the company maintains a database of registered owners, the call-tracking database should be able to access that database. Phone numbers, addresses, purchase history, and other information from registration cards should ideally already be in the database when the tech support person takes the first call from the user.

Reports and Queries

The call-tracking database described above would be of little use without some flexible report generation capabilities. Some standard reports will be produced regularly that address the following questions.

- How many calls are taken monthly about which products?

- How many calls are taken by each tech support person daily?

- When during the day are the most calls taken?

- What percentage of calls are being answered immediately?

- How many go to the next stage of support?

- What is the average call length?

- Does this length change as a result of a new product release or special training program?

In addition to these kinds of routinely produced reports, the system should allow quick queries to determine if there is recorded experience with a particular type of problem. For this kind of searching, specialized search and retrieval software may be more useful than the search capabilities of most relational database software. This type of software allows a user to specify terms in various combinations that might appear in a file. The terms can be linked in so-called Boolean relationships—"Monochrome" but *not* "Hercules," for example. These utilities also usually offer some kind of fuzzy search feature that allows searching for terms that are similar to, but not exactly the same as, some specified term. This can be valuable when searching for someone's name that isn't remembered exactly, or which might have been entered incorrectly. Some relational database software has similar features, but usually it is clumsier and more difficult than search and retrieval software. We'll look at some commercial search and retrieval software in "Commercial Information Management Software" below.

What Goes In? So much for the nuts and bolts of the call-tracking system. It's time to discuss a little about the art of writing clear and useful problem descriptions and solutions. Without some guidelines and instruction, the various tech support people who enter data into the system will develop their own individual literary styles and approaches to recording what they consider salient information. Some will be telegraphic in the extreme, others will go on for screen after screen of tedious, unimportant detail.

Though this inconsistency might not be disastrous when a problem is solved immediately, it can be when the problem must be passed on to another level of tech support. An engineer or senior tech support person generally wants more information rather than less, but what he most prefers is a concise, clear statement of all the relevant information. Just what is "relevant information" varies with each product. This is knowledge that tech support people should be taught in training and further develops during the course of answering calls. Talking to busy engineers who pointedly explain that key information has not been entered, or that the language is incomprehensible will also encourage improved descriptions.

Even if the problem is solved in the first call to tech support, the potential benefits of a call-tracking database as a knowledgebase is lost if there is no consistency to the recording of questions and answers. As discussed in Chapter 4, *Handling Support Calls,* the process of solving technical problems by phone works best when there is a consistent, rational, and yet flexible routine to the process. The recording of a problem in the call-tracking database should be part of that routine, and the form of the recording should aid the tech support person in troubleshooting.

The protocol that makes most sense is simple, and it's stolen from the oldest troubleshooting tradition—medicine.

- Briefly record the problem symptoms (or questions).

- Conduct an examination (ask questions) and record the results (answers).

- Develop a diagnosis and record it.

- Do tests to determine if the diagnosis is correct (unless you're quite sure it is). Record the test and result.

- Offer a prescription (solution, workaround, apology), and record it.

- Record the prescription results.

- If the prescription worked, indicate that call is closed. If not, get more facts, try another diagnosis, or call in a specialist (escalate).

It's fine to use abbreviations, catchwords, and specialized jargon in these records as long as everyone involved knows what they mean. Jargon can save a lot of keystrokes.

Sometimes another kind of information should be added to the record: details about the caller that are relevant to solving the problem. Is he irate? A complete novice? The president of a major corporation? Is there a language problem that makes it hard to solve the problem? Is there a crisis at the caller's workplace that makes a quick solution imperative? These human factors are important, and may aid another tech support person in the future. Needless to say, no such information should be insulting, racist, or sexist.

Some organizations have a formalized severity scale that is used to grade uncompleted calls for urgency. An example of such a scale follows.

- Severity 1—Severe impact on customer business due to product-related problem

- Severity 2—Less severe but still significant impact

- Severity 3—Reduced function without major impact

Grading calls with this scale helps those who will follow up on the uncompleted call to prioritize their work and should help to improve customer satisfaction.

User Documentation

"Have you read the manual?" Probably every tech support person who ever lived has asked that question (or wanted to) hundreds of times. At various tech support operations I've heard estimates that from 30 percent to 60 percent of the questions that come in are answered fully in the user manuals. However frustrated we become about users' refusal to read the book, it's obvious that this documentation has to be the key resource for the tech support staff, and that the staff has to know the user documentation from cover to cover. Otherwise, how will the tech be able to quickly and confidently say "Well, if you'll just look at page 68..."?

But tech support people, like other computer users, have probably had their own problems with documentation. After answering a few hundred questions that force you to search an inadequate index or tease out the meaning of unclear instructions and translate them for nontechnical users, you may develop a little more sympathy for the user.

Lamenting the shortcomings of the manuals is not enough. Support people have to deal with the manual as it is by marking errors, annotating sections that need clarification, and beefing up the index and table of contents. Each workstation should have an annotated copy of each version of the user manual for every product that is currently supported.

Manuals Online?

It's quite possible to have a version of the user manual available online on every computer in the tech support center, and to be able to do word searches of the contents, to insert comments, or to highlight important parts. While this approach might seem like an obvious improvement over reliance on paper manuals, there are some serious problems with it that should be considered. First, preparing an online version of the manual takes time and some degree of skill, and the effort will have to be repeated for each version of the documentation. Second, the manual in its paper form is what the user has in hand, and the tech is probably going to have to make reference to it often. This will be a problem if there are any significant differences between what the tech and the caller are looking at in terms of layout, pagination, or illustrative material. Third, as mentioned above, documentation in book form is often easier to handle, to read, and to find one's way in.

So, though there may well be good reasons to have the manual available online (see "The Knowledgebase" later in this chapter), it's important that each tech support person has complete paper documentation, and that documentation should be annotated thoroughly. And though each tech will have occasion to mark his own copies, it should be a department goal that important discoveries are routinely shared. If an error is found by one tech, it should be marked in all copies of the manual in the department. For this reason, among others, there should be a control list of each piece of documentation in the department and each copy should have a unique number marked on it.

It almost goes without saying that problems with the user manual discovered by the tech support staff need to be conveyed regularly to those responsible for writing the next revision.

Special Technical Documentation

There are always other types of documentation about technical products: service manuals, programmers' documentation, technical specifications, parts lists, and problem (bug) lists. This material is generally prepared and used by the engineering staff for their work in designing, servicing, and improving the products.

Whether all this material is available and useful to the tech support staff depends on a number of things, including the complexity and nature of the product, the technical expertise of the tech support staff, and the level of support being offered. There is very often an understandable hesitancy on the part of engineers to release copies of working documentation to others, especially since it was not created with that in mind. And often the engineers' documentation is not directly useful in answering the kinds of questions that come in from users. Certain kinds of technical information, like bug lists, are extremely useful to tech support people and must be supplied in some form for the operation to succeed.

The Knowledgebase

In addition to the information sources discussed so far, the tech support staff needs a manual specifically designed to help answer questions. This is different than an annotated user manual because the focus is quite different—on the tech support staff's needs, not the user's. Such a document will also become one of the primary training materials for new staff. At Computer Hand Holding, our support manual is now online, backed up by a binder containing most of the same information as well as product brochures and other printed materials on the products we support.

The information assembled here will depend greatly on the types of products being supported, but here's a list of the contents of a typical example.

Table of contents. Lays out clearly what follows, broken down into discrete sections with page numbers.

Company policies. Clearly explains all the company's policies that touch on any aspect of the tech support staff's work with callers. Scope of support offered, escalation policy, upgrade policy are all covered.

Product overview. In a page or so, gives a basic overview of the product, including basic functions, performance claims, and limitations. Diagrams are helpful here. No matter how well trained the staff, there are times when looking at such an overview will help.

Troubleshooting aids. As discussed in Chapter 4, *Handling Support Calls,* it's often possible to develop useful charts and question lists to help solve difficult problems.

Interactions. Lists all known problems/issues encountered with other software and hardware.

Most frequent problems. A large percentage of calls will generally relate to a small number of issues (the ratio often cited is 80/20, but obviously it varies with the product). Maintaining a list of those frequent questions is one of the most profitable uses for staff time. Whether the list contains ten, 100, or 1000 questions, it will need to be organized in some useful way to enable quick searching. We'll say more about this list later.

List of known problems/bugs. This should be obvious, but it's not always available. Without this list, tech support is doomed to escalate calls relating to the same bugs over and over again. The bug list has to give as much information as necessary to diagnose the bug as well as explaining when the bug will be fixed.

Version/model history. Each version of the product should be listed along with its date, features, and problems. Only the versions that are currently supported *need* to be included, but why not be complete?

Background information/glossary. All sorts of computer information could be useful here if there's room, such as other tech support phone numbers, operating system commands, ASCII tables, and definitions of various concepts. Online manuals have the potential for an almost infinite collection of more or less useful information. Someone has to input and organize it, though.

Advertising, marketing materials, and reviews. Here a binder shines over an online system (which proves you really want both). This kind of material directly helps answer questions, especially ones about published specifications, prices, etc. And people often refer to published reviews, so it's good to have them at hand.

Index/key word list. A good index is important whether the knowledgebase is online or on paper. If online, though, the index can be supplemented by word searching. Remember, indexing needs to be updated with each change in text and pagination. A good word processor with an indexing function can really help.

This list isn't exhaustive. Any number of sections could be added to help with specific products. In vertical market applications, for example, there might need to be extensive information about the business procedures or equipment the product helps support.

Unique Problems or Useful Problems? A point needs to be added about the "most frequent problems" listed above. Theoretically, it's possible to develop a list of *every* unique problem that comes into the tech support center. Such a list could be derived from an analysis of questions and answers in the call-tracking database, put into some organized form and made available online. Would the resulting knowledgebase become a powerful resource for the staff, worth the time spent developing it? Maybe, but many problems that come to tech support are pretty unique to the caller, results of misunderstandings, unusual hardware, or strange software interactions. More practical than keeping a list of every unique problem, then, would be a process whereby every call record is analyzed to glean *useful* information.

Some commercial call-tracking systems (such as SupportWise by BusinessWise discussed below) have a feature that allows some call reports to be flagged as "interesting." When the call is completed, the support person makes a judgment as to whether the call represents a significant, new piece of information that should be made available in the organization's knowledgebase.

Alert System

So far, we've talked entirely about systems for collecting and accessing information, but there is another part of the equation that needs to be mentioned. A system should be in place to ensure that information gets to the affected staff in a timely way. Specifically, some form of alert procedure is necessary to communicate important information to tech support staff immediately and clearly. When a new and serious bug is discovered, this information must be communicated to everyone. This alert system might be something as mundane as a bulletin board (which everyone regularly reads) for late-breaking information. It might be an alert memo on colored paper that goes to every affected staff person. Or it might be an electronic mail message that flashes on every workstation screen as soon as it is powered up in the morning.

Whatever medium the alert system is based on, it's important to keep a paper record of all support alerts that have been distributed. Giving each alert a unique number makes it much easier to keep track of them and refer to them later. Each support person can then keep a consecutive file of alerts for future reference.

Technical Library

As a workplace devoted to helping people with technology, a

tech support center needs a library of technical literature to support it in its mission. Technical literature on the hardware and software environment our products work in is vital, and the only way to make the books, pamphlets, magazines, and software really useful is to keep it organized in a library. In most tech support centers having a full-fledged librarian would be overkill, but some kind of system for keeping the stuff in order is important. You don't need an M.L.S. degree to get the job done, but you do need four basics.

- A classification system. This just means a way to arrange the materials on the shelf so that someone knows where to look for them.

- A numbering system. Numbers that reflects the classification system and which can be marked on the materials in the library help you know where to put the books.

- A check-out system. When someone takes something a check-out system provides a way to track it down. This might be as simple as a sheet of paper. It might just be a policy like "Use it here!"

- A librarian. Every system needs someone who keeps all the above in order, and who puts the stuff back on the shelf when others don't.

I don't think most tech support centers need a catalog for their library. It wouldn't hurt, but keeping a real catalog in shape is a bigger job than you might think.

Classification systems for a small computer library ought to be fairly easy to develop. The existing library classification systems like the Library of Congress and Dewey systems are overly complicated, and probably don't reflect the way the literature is used in a support organization. At Computer Hand Holding we keep our small library semi-organized in roughly the following order.

A. General (reference books, directories, etc.)
B. Software
    1. Operating systems
    2. Programming languages

3. Applications
    a) Word processing
    b) Database
    c) Spreadsheets
    d) Graphics
    e) Telecommunications
4. Utilities
C. Hardware
    1. CPU
    2. Peripherals
    3. Interfacing
D. Miscellaneous

It's simple but it works. We keep our software collection in the same shelves, next to any associated literature. Coming up with a classification system that works for a small library requires a little thought and some time with an outline processor. Don't get too fancy. If there's more than a couple of shelves to organize, hire a specialist!

Hypertext and Expert Systems

Two flashy though not exactly new information technologies are beginning to make themselves felt these days, hypertext and expert systems. Both offer many possibilities for creating powerful online systems that can provide the support person with key information to help solve users' problems. Later on in this chapter, we look at some products that incorporate these technologies, but a brief description of their basic concepts is in order here.

Hypertext. Hypertext is a form of online information system where discrete pieces of related data are linked together so that the user can quickly go back and forth between them. A simple hypertext system might show a screenful of text about a product with certain important terms in the text highlighted. The user can move the cursor to those terms, hit a key, and instantly view a definition of the highlighted term. Hypertext can include images as well as text. For example, a picture of the product might appear on the screen, and again the user could move the cursor to a part of the product, press a button, and instantly view a technical description of the part. Hypertext systems can be much more complex than these examples, of course. You could jump from the picture to a text and then to another text or picture, and so on.

The potential usefulness of hypertext for tech support is obvious. The support person could have access to a hypertext system that contains all available technical information about the products he supports, including images and diagrams. Using a mouse he could navigate through the text and images, finding the information he needs to solve the problem without fumbling with a bunch of paper documents. Without discounting this potential, however, the problem with hypertext is that someone has to carefully design and implement it, creating all those links between data elements. Without planning and care, the user can easily get lost in a maze of text and images.

Expert systems. Expert systems are programs that do what a human expert does: use knowledge and reasoning to perform a difficult task. Expert systems are often designed to do just what a tech support person does: troubleshoot problems. Like the human troubleshooter, the expert system would present a series of questions about the problem to a user. The user answers the questions and the answers cause the expert system to pose appropriate new questions, until the system has enough information to make a recommendation about how to solve the problem.

Creating an expert system that can really solve significant problems is no small feat. Different approaches are being tried, but generally the task involves breaking the problem-solving process down into a series of logical rules. Expert system developers, often called "knowledge engineers," spend a lot of their time interviewing human experts to determine what factors they consider when solving problems. Think about how many rules would be necessary to diagnose all the problems that occur with the products you support and you'll get a sense of how hard it would be to have an expert system replace you. Often, though, expert systems are employed to deal with a considerably reduced subset of possible problems. They might be used to help configure complicated systems, for example.

Expert systems are already being used by a number of companies in real world troubleshooting situations, and tech support is likely to be increasingly involved in putting them to practical use. Off-the-shelf expert systems are beginning to be marketed that can troubleshoot specific computer systems. The benefits in terms of shorter training time and more uniform quality are too important to ignore, though the challenges are significant.

Hybrid systems. A number of products are available that combine elements of hypertext with expert system technology to provide the best features of both. With these products you could create an online system containing technical documentation for a product complete with hypertext links. The system would also contain a troubleshooting module that you could invoke as needed. Alternatively, you could create an expert system and add hypertext to help clarify technical details. Hypertext and expert systems are also being used as "intelligent front ends" to traditional database systems.

An Evolving Information Management System

At Computer Hand Holding, we've built a call-tracking database and knowledgebase out of a combination of off-the-shelf products and internally developed applications. We call the system TechTalk. The process of its evolution might be instructive to other support operations interested in creating a custom solution tailored to their own needs rather than buying a complete, ready-made support software package.

When Emil Flock started Computer Hand Holding in 1983, he needed a tool that would help him keep track of the calls he was taking. If there were any adaptable "off-the-shelf" call-tracking systems at that point, they were probably beyond the means of a fledgling company with two employees.

Call tracking. What was needed seemed fairly simple: a database system that would allow entry of the caller's name and phone number, system configuration, question and answer fields, call status (completed or not), and, not least, the length of the call. This information would be vital to keeping clients informed about the types of problems their customers were reporting. And call length was crucial information for billing purposes. At this stage, no attempt was made to integrate a knowledgebase component into the system.

Flock was an avid Paradox database programmer and he used that product to construct the call-tracking system. Paradox's relative ease of use made creating and improving the call-tracking application a lot less time consuming than it might have been. It's also pretty easy for support staff to do queries of the database without programming.

As Computer Hand Holding went from one PC in the beginning to a Novell network with eight workstations sharing access to the database, Paradox has been able to keep pace. It allows multiple users to use the same database, locking records currently in use. A recently released version, Paradox 3.5, has drastically improved the speed of the system.

TechTalk's user interface revolves around two main screens. The operator first encounters the "header screen" where the caller's name, phone number, system configuration, and company name/address (if important) are entered (see Figure 5-1). Then the operator goes to the "question/answer screen," where the crux of the call is entered (see Figure 5-2). On exiting, the support person can enter a classification number that describes the type of call and indicate if the call is completed or not. Uncompleted call records are sent to a queue where they're held for further action. They're also printed out.

Online knowledgebase. As Computer Hand Holding grew, adding employees and developing a considerable body of written documentation about the products it supports, it became clear that an online knowledgebase was needed to share the information and keep it updated. Adding the knowledgebase to the Paradox call-tracking application was one option, but not an easy one. Database systems like Paradox are great for structured information that can fit into fixed-length fields but much less adaptable to freeform textual information like tech notes. Including desirable hypertext functions would be nearly impossible.

The solution came in the form of a modest but powerful piece of software called XHelp by Exwells Software of Oakland, Cali-

Figure 5-1

TechTalk's header screen

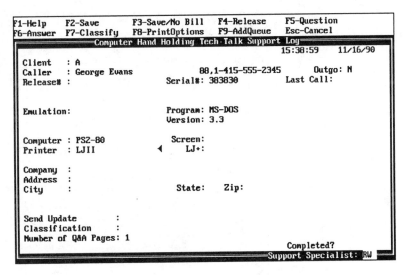

Figure 5-2

TechTalk's question/answer screen

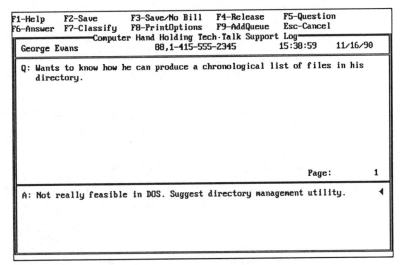

fornia. This pop-up information system allows instant access to any text that's been entered into it (see Figure 5-3). Information in XHelp is organized according to a booklike metaphor. A table of contents at the beginning of the text shows the structure of the information. From there, hitting a key can take you to any "page" of the file, or you may browse the material page by page. A word search capability constitutes the index of the book. In addition, hypertext links can be used to connect any word in a text to related material elsewhere.

Figure 5-3

Exwells's

XHelp screen

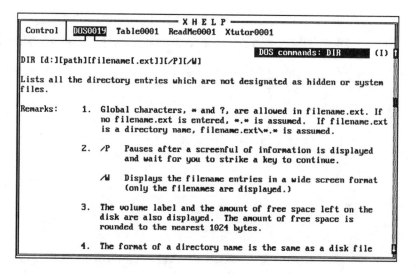

Creating a useful and well-organized XHelp text requires some care but it's not difficult. Keeping screens of information uncluttered is important. It's better to have many sparse pages than fewer crammed ones. Experience shows it's better to keep the number of hypertext links down to a reasonable number. Support people working online with callers don't have the time and attention to follow convoluted paths to the information they need.

Multitasking. The next step in TechTalk's evolution was multitasking. First using DesqView by Quarterdeck Office Systems and later Microsoft Windows 3, we've been able to add the ability to switch easily between the TechTalk system and the software we support, and back again, while taking a call. Although we still use XHelp for our online knowledgebase, having a stable multitasking environment opens up many new information possibilities that we're just beginning to explore.

TechTalk's ability to grow and integrate with other software has been its strength. Dividing the call-tracking component (the Paradox application) from the knowledgebase component (XHelp) has brought some benefits, namely, both sides of the equation can do what they do best. Multitasking is a major addition, making the system even more flexible. Though we're a ways short of the ideal system described below, we have a working support tool that handles the basics and still has room to grow.

Questions for do-it-yourselfers. Building our own system has been no snap. It's hard to estimate the time we've invested in it, and there have been plenty of frustrations. Now, though, we have a powerful tool that's well adapted to the way we work, and one that we can improve further in the future. Other organizations thinking about developing inhouse solutions to their call-tracking and knowledgebase needs might consider a few of the following questions.

- Do you have staff resources to develop the application properly?

- Can you do the systems design homework to create the right system for your organization?

- Can you cope with the length of the development project, or do you need a working system *now*?

- If you're trying to save money by building your own system, does a realistic assessment of the costs involved really show any savings over commercial products?

- Have you really looked at what's available?

The Ideal Tech Support Information Tool

A number of companies have begun offering specialized software products to fill the information needs of support operations. In "Commercial Information Management Software" we'll look at a number of those products, but before going shopping or even reading product literature I recommend doing some serious brainstorming within your organization about just what you want and need in the way of information tools. Your support group works differently than any other and has its own unique approach, so you ought to develop your own ideas about what constitutes the ideal information tool before choosing a ready-made solution or building your own. Even if you already have some kind of support software in place, there's a good chance that you've gained enough experience with it to begin thinking about how it could be improved, especially if you've had it for a while.

At Computer Hand Holding we have an information system that works well for us as discussed above. Recently, though, we spent some time thinking about the features of an ideal, next-generation system, relatively unconstrained by the limitations of our present technology. Here is the profile of our ideal system.

- Integrated, it combines call tracking, knowledgebase, online documentation, electronic mail, etc.

- Tracks people, calls, problems, system configurations.

- Has a graphic interface and allows free use of images and diagrams.

- Automatically "learns" (adds to the knowledgebase) as questions and answers are entered into the call-tracking system.

- "Self-organizing," it uses automatic methods to make information easy to access.

- Contains remote access features to allow direct connection to a caller's system.

- Works smoothly on our network system.

- Allows smooth routing of information to interested parties.

- Multitasking, allowing easy movement between call tracking and any other computer operation.

- Has intelligent (expert system) features to help guide the tech through the process of helping callers.

Our brainstorming session was useful and informative. No support software yet offers everything on our wish list, but developing it made us better able to evaluate what's available and think about how to improve our present system.

Commercial Information Management Software

In this section we'll look at some software products that are available now and are already being used for tech support. I won't try to provide rigorous reviews here, and "Commercial Information Management Software" should definitely *not* be taken as an endorsement of specific products. Instead I want to suggest some of the directions software developers have taken in their attempts to help support departments with their formidable information challenges.

Included are five products, covering integrated call-tracking and online information systems as well as tools for text retrieval and electronic publishing, expert systems, and hypertext development. The focus is on microcomputer products.

SupportWise: Integrated Support Software

SupportWise combines call tracking and knowledgebase in a package that's designed to fit smoothly into the work patterns of tech support operations. Written in Progress, SupportWise operates in a range of environments including MS-DOS, UNIX, XENIX, and DEC-VMS. Up to 30 workstations are supported in the PC-LAN version. Larger computer versions allow unlimited workstations. SupportWise is unique in being a full-featured software application designed specifically for tech support on a range of widely used hardware platforms.

SupportWise emphasizes what it calls event tracking rather than cutting-edge knowledgebase technology. You won't find hypertext, expert systems, or other artificial intelligence features included in this package, though there are several powerful tools for accessing a range of tech support information resources. Event tracking includes the ability to document a specific customer, call, case, or action, and to have the system keep users informed of the status of each. A call is, of course, a specific contact; a case, about which one or a number of calls might come in, is a specific problem; and an action is something someone must do in response to a particular case. SupportWise has numerous report formats that monitor performance and show the status of cases and actions.

The heart of the SupportWise system is the call-processing screen, which BusinessWise chose to make as uncluttered as possible (see Figure 5-4). You can make text fields of unlimited length and add custom fields as needed. This is where you enter callers' names, and check them automatically against lists of registered users or contract holders.

Figure 5-4

SupportWise's call-processing screen

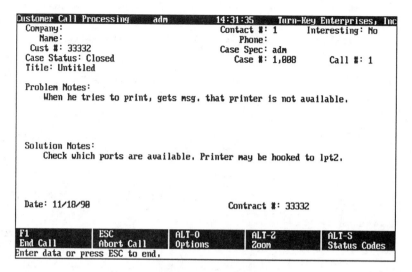

```
Customer Call Processing    adm        14:31:35    Turn-Key Enterprises, Inc
  Company:                            Contact #: 1      Interesting: No
     Name:                              Phone:
   Cust #: 33332                     Case Spec: adm
Case Status: Closed                      Case #: 1,000    Call #: 1
  Title: Untitled

Problem Notes:
    When he tries to print, gets msg. that printer is not available.




Solution Notes:
    Check which ports are available. Printer may be hooked to lpt2.




Date: 11/18/90                       Contract #: 33332



F1                ESC              ALT-O         ALT-Z         ALT-S
End Call          Abort Call       Options       Zoom          Status Codes
Enter data or press ESC to end.
```

You enter problems and solutions on the call-processing screen and from here you can access other information and features by hitting a couple of keys. You can browse previous calls from this caller at any time or you can flag calls as "interesting," meaning they're informative for one reason or another.

During a call, the operator can hit a key to consult Tech Notes, the SupportWise online technical information medium. Searching Tech Notes involves typing in key words, which can be combined for a Boolean search of available topics. On request, a list of active key words and the number of "hits" for each appears on the screen to show you which terms are likely to find useful information. Tech notes are usually added by an administrator, who may take the information from call reports flagged by techs as "interesting" (see Figure 5-5), or they may be created from scratch using a built-in editor. Key words are selected for each tech note as it's entered.

After a call is finished, a post call-processing screen allows you to adjust the call's timing—to account for offline research or an interruption, for example—and to classify the call using any codes established by the support organization (see Figure 5-6). The system can keep track of time against the terms of a service contract.

SupportWise supports call queuing. Caller information can be entered by receptionists or dispatchers for later handling, and spe-

Figure 5-5
*SupportWise's
interesting call screen*

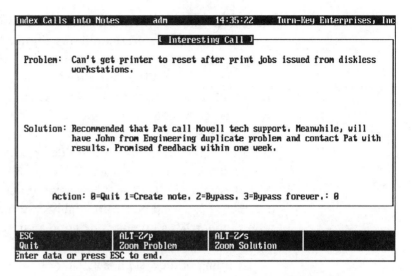

Figure 5-6
*Support-
Wise's postcall-
processing screen*

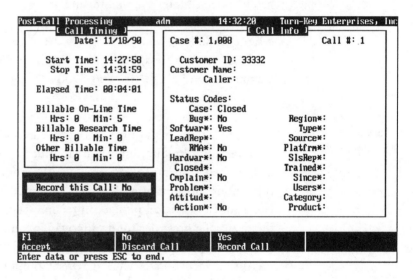

cific queues can be maintained for different individuals or work groups. Queued calls can be given priority ratings to aid techs in selecting which to take first.

SupportWise's Action Items feature lets you enter required actions so that the system will track them until completed—sort of an automated to-do list. A call might trigger an action item like "Send Patch #121 to Sally Meyer." Action items can be routed to any other SupportWise user on the network. Action items are marked to indicate when they should be done as well as who is responsible. This feature should make it much harder for promised actions to "slip through the cracks."

A nice SupportWise feature is the message board for communication between individuals on the system as well as for posting messages to all users. This device makes it easy to broadcast important news to everyone instantly.

SupportWise is a product that's designed from scratch for customer support, and it shows. Priced in the neighborhood of $1000 per user in its PC-LAN version (prices vary according to number of users and platform), highly customizable, and available now, SupportWise presents one good argument against trying to build your own tech support application. The only obvious shortcoming of the system is its rather limited knowledgebase capability. Tech Notes is a fine feature as far as it goes, but it would be great to add other features like hypertext and, perhaps, expert system modules.

Contact BusinessWise, 595 Millich Drive, Suite 210, Campbell, CA 95008, 408-866-5960 for more information.

. . . .

Apriori: Innovative Knowledge Access

Answer Computer's apriori software, currently running on Sun hardware, is a unique, high-end attempt to answer the question of how best to capture and organize the ongoing experience of the support organization. Answer Computer was founded by the late Tom Evans, a real pioneer in technical support, and apriori is the result of a great deal of his innovative thinking about the fundamentals of the business.

Apriori incorporates what Answer Computer calls an "experience-based learning engine." As problem and solution notes are entered into the system they become part of an ever-growing body of shared knowledge. As other support people respond to the same problems they can find the solutions recorded in the knowledgebase.

Apriori keeps track of the frequency of reported problems and regularly reorders the problem/solution list so that the most commonly encountered are always at the top. The idea of this "bubble up" process is that the support person will find the most useful information at the head of the list without wading through tons of less–likely solutions (see Figure 5-7). What the support person actually sees in the list is a stack of numbered, one-line descriptions of problems. When one looks promising the support person points and clicks on the heading to get the full description of the problem and solution. The description can contain text, graphic images, or application code.

When a new problem comes along that the support person can't answer and that's not yet in the system, apriori routes the caller's configuration and symptom information to a specialist who works on the problem and enters a solution directly into the system. A complete audit trail allows tracing the progress of the reported problem from first report to its solution.

The benefits of such a self-organizing system are obvious. Every support person is constantly adding to the knowledgebase and the system itself keeps the information in an accessible structure. Unlike an expert system or most hypertext information systems, there's no need for any programming or elaborate design for the structure of the information. This doesn't mean that the system can be fully effective without some initial setup. Normally, a system administrator will enter some information into the system first, most likely by importing the documentation and technical

Figure 5-7
Apriori's "bubble up" screen

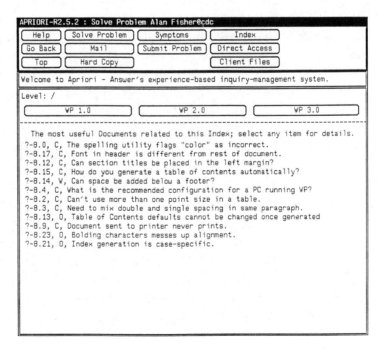

notes of the supported product and dividing it into problem/solution chunks. Apriori also allows the full text of any product documentation to be instantly available online.

Augmenting the "bubble up" lists of all the most common problems described above, apriori supports other ways to search for answers. Symptoms matching a caller's problem can be sought through a search of key word indexes maintained in the system. Problems can also be searched in a narrowed list broken down by topics, which are, of course, customizable. Apriori allows hypertext-like "Also see" links to be created between any problem description and related entries anywhere in the system.

Less flashy but equally important as the innovative technical information technology described above are the functions apriori includes to log individual calls. The system tracks callers' names, organizations, service terms, and system configurations, and a history of all contacts and status of open issues is instantly available to the support person or manager. Reports can be generated to show problem frequencies, durations, and types, as well as support personnel performance and other support center statistics. Apriori can be told to automatically notify affected users when a new solution or update is available.

Esther Dyson, writing in the newsletter *Release 1.0* (July 13, 1989), wrote, "Apriori makes most sense where there are complex products that come in many versions, with a solution set too broad to be known thoroughly by any single person." That includes, of course, many of the high-end software products that run on Sun computers. The first apriori customer was Interleaf, for the support of its high-end Technical Publishing System software.

Though Answer Computer expects to make apriori available on other platforms, its current restriction as a Sun-based system limits its immediate usefulness to most support operations. Nonetheless, apriori's innovative approach to support information should make it interesting to anyone in the business.

For more information contact Answer Computer, Inc., 1263 Oakmead Parkway, Sunnyvale, CA 94086, 408-739-6130.

Views: Smart Text Retrieval

Folio Corporation's Folio Views is a product for MS-DOS machines that combines elements of text search and retrieval software, hypertext, word processing, and electronic publishing and then adds a new twist called underhead technology so the whole will be smaller than the sum of the parts. Underhead means that after entering text into Views and indexing it, the resulting files will be smaller than the original by as much as 50 percent.

WordPerfect uses Views to help its support people access the large amounts of technical reference material used to support its products. Before Views, WordPerfect issued black binders filled with tech notes to its hundreds of reps, and of course, that meant constantly updating the binders as information needed to be added and changed.

To use Views, text files such as product documentation and tech notes are broken down into chunks, usually paragraphs, by the insertion of a special character at the beginning of each chunk. Views calls these chunks "folios." Then the text is processed by Views, first to compress the data and then to index it. Indexing can take a long time for multimegabyte text collections. But unlike other text retrieval software, Views lets you modify your text—annotate it using the Views word processor, for example, or add more entries—without having to reindex the whole knowledgebase.

Indexing allows Views to retrieve text almost instantaneously. Just about as fast as you can type a word, Views can present all the folios containing the text, each in a different window on screen. Naturally, terms can be combined in complex searches and wildcards may be used. The resulting searches are still very fast.

Every time you do a search, the collection of retrieved folios is called a "view" (see Figure 5-8). A view can also be a collection of folios which you've grouped together because they contain related information. Either way, a view can be preserved for later reference by giving it a name.

To guide users through all these views and folios it can be handy to have an old-fashioned table of contents. The software lets you create one and link each entry with associated folios by way of hypertext links. Links can also be used to connect any word in any folio with any related folio, to clarify a concept, for example. You jump between linked folios by hitting the tab key.

Once your support center creates a useful knowledgebase of technical information, you're ready to become an electronic

Figure 5-8

*A view from
Folio Views*

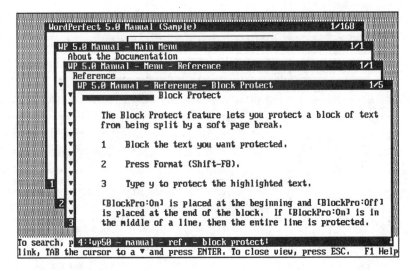

publisher. Folio produces an inexpensive runtime version called Previews that can be distributed with your knowledgebases. Novell has for some time been distributing Netware documentation to all its customers as a Views knowledgebase using Previews. WordPerfect and other software companies seem to be following suit. In fact, Folio seems to have created a standard for electronic publishing that's being used by a diverse array of customers. Specialists advertise their services in Folio's newsletter as Views developers.

Getting back to tech support, WordPerfect reports being happy with the way Views has superseded those thick black binders. Linked by a network of 11 file servers, over 500 support reps may now consult a different knowledgebase for each WordPerfect product. Opening menus with options like Features, Printers, Installation, etc., lead the technician to more detailed menus and from there to relevant folios. At any time the tech can do a word search to find useful text anywhere in the system.

Making reams of paper documentation fit smoothly into this new medium took some work. Initially, a group of editors in the customer support information center verified and corrected material in the old binders, entered it into the knowledgebases, and then created the menu links. WordPerfect says it adds 100 to 150 new pieces of information into the knowledgebases weekly.

Even support centers that don't answer 10,000 calls a day like WordPerfect might take a close look at Views as a tool for creating online information resources. Of course, Views doesn't contain a call-tracking component, so it couldn't be the complete answer for most operations. But used in conjunction with a multitasking environment like DesqView or Windows and a suitable call-tracking database, Views could provide a powerful support tool, and it could get the support center into the business of electronically publishing some of its valuable information, which is a business with a future.

Contact Folio Corporation, 2155 North Freedom Blvd., Suite 200, Provo, UT 84604, 801-375-3700.

KnowledgePro: Online Information Language

KnowledgePro by Knowledge Garden, Inc. represents a unique development tool for MS-DOS computers incorporating hypertext and expert system features. It's designed to enable development of intelligent online information systems, such as documentation of complex procedures or processes, or automated tutorials. Tech support centers could use it to build systems for accessing a knowledgebase, incorporating hypertext to link related information, and adding expert system features to aid troubleshooting.

KnowledgePro attempts to solve some of the shortcomings of both hypertext and expert systems. Hypertext systems generally suffer from not being controllable—there's usually no way to lead a user through the network of linked information or to respond to input by the user. On the other hand, expert systems require too much control, too much explicit definition of every factor required to reach a solution. This makes expert systems painfully slow and expensive to develop and has limited their overall usefulness. KnowledgePro lets developers simply present information, collect input, and use expert system rules when appropriate (see Figure 5-9).

KnowledgePro is really a simple but powerful programming language that can be used to present text, ask questions requiring user input, implement expert system functions, and link to other programs, data files (including dBase and 1-2-3 files), and graphic

Figure 5-9

KnowledgePro's
expert system

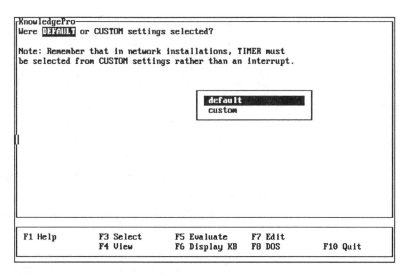

```
┌KnowledgePro──────────────────────────────────────────────────────
│Were DEFAULT or CUSTOM settings selected?
│
│Note: Remember that in network installations, TIMER must
│be selected from CUSTOM settings rather than an interrupt.
│
│
│
│                              ┌─────────────────────────┐
│                              │ default                 │
│                              │ custom                  │
│                              └─────────────────────────┘
│
│
│
│
│
│
│
│
│
├──────────────────────────────────────────────────────────────────
│ F1 Help        F3 Select     F5 Evaluate    F7 Edit
│                F4 View       F6 Display KB  F8 DOS        F10 Quit
└──────────────────────────────────────────────────────────────────
```

images. Versions of KnowledgePro allow it to control CD-ROM and laser disk hardware, and a new version called KPWin is available to build knowledge systems in Windows.

One of the KnowledgePro commands you might employ is SAY. You might create a directive as simple as SAY('THIS IS A TROUBLESHOOTING SYSTEM.'). This command puts the text on the screen and leaves it there until the user hits the space bar. By inserting some codes around a term or phrase, a hypertext link can be made to another text, an entire file, or even another program. Most often, hypertext will probably be used to give further information about a word or phrase on screen.

Another command is ASK, which allows a question to be asked of the user. The user is then provided with a menu of possible answers, an editor screen to write a paragraph reply, or a blank for a single word. Control is available over what kinds of input are allowed and default replies can be set. A support person could use an editing window to describe a caller's problem and menus to match their configuration, for example. KnowledgePro also has search features that could look for words from the description in a large knowledgebase of previous problems.

Creating useful knowledgebases requires more than mastering the nuts and bolts of KnowledgePro. There's usually a fair amount of thinking and planning required before the information that needs to be communicated can be put into KnowledgePro.

This might best be done with paper and pencil as the builder finds ways to diagram, flow chart, or storyboard the process that will be presented to the ultimate user. This design phase might be the most valuable part of the whole process of creating an information system, since it helps clarify and systematize the information you're trying to communicate.

KnowledgePro provides tools that could be used to create a complete tech support system, including call tracking, technical knowledgebase, and diagnostic features. It would have the advantage over existing systems of being completely customizable. Disadvantages might include speed of operation and, perhaps, lack of record locking and other network features. Building such a system would hardly be a trivial task, but would be within the capabilities of many tech support organizations. More likely this software would be used in conjunction with a database application, which would handle call tracking while KnowledgePro provided the knowledgebase component of a complete support center software package. KnowledgePro could also be used for more specialized tasks, like building tech support tutorials and specialized diagnostic systems. If a tech support center is ready to start building its own knowledgebase systems, KnowledgePro is a good tool to look at.

Contact Knowledge Garden, Inc., 473A Malden Bridge Rd., Nassau, NY 12123, 518-766-3000.

Mahogony HelpDesk: Automated Expert System Builder

For years, people have been wondering when expert system technology would be able to help out in tech support. The stumbling block has been the difficulty of developing any system that's "smart" enough to really help. Mahogony HelpDesk by Emerald Intelligence is designed to make the development process as simple as possible so that you can actually get an expert system built before the product it troubleshoots is obsolete.

Running on Apple Macintoshes and MS-DOS computers under Microsoft Windows, Mahogony HelpDesk is really a suite of separately sold component programs. HelpBuilder allows you to build your system by using a mouse to create a hierarchy of symptoms and solutions. The network of nodes representing your expert system quickly takes shape on your screen, and you use the mouse to make links between elements. A popup editor lets you write and revise diagnostic questions and quickly build menus for user input.

HelpStation is a runtime system that lets users access the expert system created with HelpBuilder. Using the system involves clicking on your responses to the diagnostic questions it presents. As you answer each question, an icon appears around the edge of the screen indicating the result. You can return to a previous point in the diagnostic dialogue by clicking on one of these icons and revising your answer to the question. Questions can be in the form of graphics, allowing you to click on part of the picture to indicate your response. While in a help session, you can access a diagram of the hierarchy of diagnostic nodes in the system and the path your answers have traced will be highlighted (see Figure 5-10). A log is maintained of all help sessions.

Optional modules for HelpDesk are HelpManager and HelpDesk Customizer. HelpManager helps you analyze information collected during HelpDesk sessions, letting you track the frequency of specific problems, for example. Customizer lets you modify the Mahogony expert system program that underlies HelpDesk, adding interfaces to databases and other software, gathering input from sensors, or operating devices such as laser disks or fax machines.

Mahogony HelpDesk is a slick product that makes building and using expert systems look easy. Of course, there's still a lot of

Figure 5-10

Mahogony Help Desk's expert system

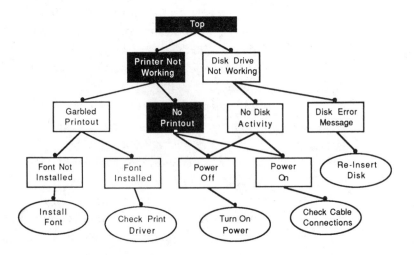

thinking to do before you can decide just what questions will lead to the right solutions, but this program greatly simplifies the mechanics of building the system. Support departments have lots of other things to do with their time.

Contact Emerald Intelligence, 3915-A1 Research Park Drive, Ann Arbor, Michigan 48108, 313-663-8757.

Managing Memory

The bane of tech support is a problem that has to be solved more than once, a question that has to be researched again and again. The support organization must aggressively develop information tools so that whenever something new is learned by one individual, it's quickly made available to everyone else. A number of different information tools are required, including a call-tracking system to document all calls and a knowledgebase of key support information. Technology is creating new methods of acquiring, organizing, and accessing the kind of technical knowledge that support centers need, and the number of commercial support tools is rapidly increasing. More important than any special information technology, though, is the commitment and discipline to develop the organization's collective memory.

Alternative Methods of Support

People helping people with technology—that's technical support. Up to now, it's mostly meant the classic hotline connection between one support person—the product expert—and one customer. It's an expensive and, many would say, inefficient way to deliver service. The search is on for ways to use technology to deliver solutions to customers more cheaply, quickly, and conveniently. No one seems to think automation will be replacing the trained support person any time soon, but many companies are finding ways to augment their telephone hotline services with alternate modes of support. They're offering online support services, machine-readable support knowledgebases, fax, automated telephone voice response, and remote control software as ways for customers to get help without the common trials of busy phone lines and long waits on hold.

Ashton-Tate is an example. Because they think of electronic support as so much more efficient than standard telephone calls, they go out of their way to make it available to customers. Buy one of their products and you receive a well-produced *Support and Services Guide* containing a precall checklist, support phone numbers, and descriptions of premium support plans as well as each of their alternative support modes, such as inhouse computer bulletin board (with 800 number), CompuServe and GEnie services, a voice response system to give answers to common questions (on Multimate, also an 800 number), a fax number you can use to send questions, and a list of their technical bulletins.

Not everyone agrees that a headlong leap into electronic support is the way to go. They argue that something is lost when a computer screen or an automated voice takes the place of a human being who can offer some t.l.c. along with the technical information. Deborah Fain, support veteran and president of Lysis Corporation, makes this point strongly. "These are our customers! Why are we trying not to talk to them? Why are we trying to find a way to get computers to talk to them?" Yet she and most other observers agree that support alternatives have their place. The trick will be to figure out just what that place is. Users seem willing to adopt new approaches when they have something to gain, just as they did when ATMs were introduced as a banking alternative.

In this chapter we'll survey a number of support alternatives. Some, like bulletin board support, are well-established, routinely taking thousands of support questions a month in many companies. Others, like voice response systems, are new—already in active service—but not making a major impact—yet.

Online Support

Online support on information utilities like CompuServe or inhouse bulletin board systems is the most widely used alternative to the old-fashioned support call. Using modem-equipped computers, users send questions and receive answers without ever hearing a busy signal, sitting on hold, or talking to anyone. They can also upload problematic files or download software patches without recourse to the U.S. Postal System, which online communicators refer to as "Snail Mail."

While working on this chapter, I had a pleasant lesson in just how smoothly online support could work. When I discovered a conflict between the latest update of my word processor and the version of the expanded memory manager I was using, I figured I was in for at least one tedious support call and probably two. And I assumed I'd have to wait until the next day during business hours to make the call(s). But instead of calling the software or computer manufacturer to see if they knew the reason for the conflict, I dialed up the latter's bulletin board, which is available 24 hours a day. Within 10 minutes I'd found the latest version of the expanded memory software, downloaded and installed it, and checked that the solution worked. No one in tech support had to take my call, find a solution, or mail me the updated software, and I was back to work with minimal delay. Not even the best "human" technical support could have produced such a quick and elegant solution.

That example is admittedly an ideal case for online support, since I didn't require troubleshooting help and already had an idea what I needed. If human assistance were required, I'd have been able to post a message with my problem and probably get an answer, but the resolution would have been much less immediate. Great as it can be, online support is no panacea.

A Little History The use of online computer communications to provide technical support started in the late sixties with the government's Advanced Research Project Agency network. This network, still in use, was created to allow vendors to answer technical questions and provide fixes to programmers and scientists working on government projects.

Later, the development of microcomputer bulletin board system (BBS) software and the public online systems it fostered provided a new communication medium for PC users that was quickly adopted to exchange technical information informally and distribute software. The first microcomputer BBSs were nonprofit operations, but soon high-tech and other companies began offering their own inhouse BBSs to provide customer service, answer technical questions, receive customer files and provide software fixes. Useful though they are, such BBSs have some inherent limitations. They can handle only a relatively small number of incoming lines and they require callers to pay long distance charges unless they happen to be in the same city, or the service provider is willing to install toll-free service.

In the late seventies, large commercial online information networks became available to microcomputer users equipped with modems by local call from most cities in the U.S. The largest of these "information utilities," CompuServe, currently has about half a million subscribers around the world. Other networks, like GEnie, Prodigy, Connect, Delphi, and BIX, are smaller than CompuServe in terms of the number of subscribers, but they may offer certain advantages, like price, ease of use, or technical focus.

Large computer software and hardware vendors were fairly quick to use these systems to offer customers a place to get the latest information about their products, check lists of most frequently asked questions, pose new questions, offer feedback, and search libraries for software patches, utilities, macros, and templates.

Lots of Pluses

The advantages are obvious. Instead of trying to handle a flood of calls for help coming in all at once, many of which are routine questions asked over and over again, your customers use their computers and modems to contact you through online information services like CompuServe, or your own inhouse bulletin board. Instead of putting your support people through the stress of dealing with harried callers on the phone all day, with problems coming at them from all directions, let them calmly read users' questions and compose answers using the company's information resources. In addition to being a kinder, gentler way for your folks to work, there's also a leverage effect. Questions and answers posted on the online system are available to all users in the future, thereby heading off calls.

Another advantage of online support is that experts and power users outside of the manufacturer's staff are often logged on and available to answer questions even before the support staff gets to them. Borland International actively enlists outside expert users, offering their "Team Borland" members free online time and other incentives in return for their active participation in providing online support. Obviously, getting some of your products' most knowledgeable users involved pays many intangible dividends beyond the obvious help and insight they provide.

And Some Minuses

Online support isn't likely to replace regular hotline support any time soon. One problem is that relatively few computer users seem to be comfortable with telecommunications. Only one half million out of the millions of microcomputer users are signed up with CompuServe, the largest of the networks, an indication that only a technically elite fraction of customers will go online when they have problems.

On the other hand, that technical elite can be sizable enough to put a big demand on your online system. One large computer manufacturer, AST, decided that answering questions on its BBS was taking so much time that it needed to change its format. The company now uses its BBS to post the most common questions and answers taken by its hotline (along with updates and patches) rather than fielding new problems from online users.

When the vendor does try to answer questions online, the response is usually not blazingly quick. Most companies shoot for 24-hour response time for new questions, which is just not fast enough for users whose work is halted because of a technical problem. There's no inherent reason why online support couldn't be nearly as fast as regular voice calls, but that would mean, once again, filling chairs with lots of techs to handle busy periods and therefore negate one of the big advantages of online services.

Online systems are also handicapped by their user interfaces, which, though changing, are still pretty stark and minimal, and by the methods used to organize and present technical information. Deborah Fain, president of Lysis Corporation, a developer of support software, finds CompuServe an awkward medium for support.

I get irritated because it takes so long to find an answer. I think they've purposely made the access methodology cumbersome and slow because they're charging me for how slow it is. I think if they were really serious about being a true information resource they would look at some of the newer access methods. Microsoft's knowledgebase works differently than the rest of CompuServe, and that's an improvement over the rest of it, but it's still not anywhere near where it should be for a state-of-the-art information system.

Fain doubts that most users will be opting for online support anytime soon. "An ordinary person," she says, "is very intimidated by telecommunications and they'll be even more intimidated by

CompuServe, particularly when it takes them twenty minutes to find an answer. A telephone call should only take them three or four minutes, and they talk to a human being."

I share some of Fain's frustration with the medium. Newer communications software, some of it specialized for use with specific services, seems to make the process somewhat easier, faster, and cheaper, but the organization of the information itself seems unnecessarily clumsy, and at CompuServe's $12.80 an hour access charge, clumsy ends up meaning expensive.

Intangible Differences

The experience of getting help online is quite different from calling a human support person. The impersonality of the process could be either positive or negative, depending on whether the user wants the human contact that a phone conversation provides. When I call a support hotline, I find explaining a problem and making sure I'm understood can be a tedious, frustrating process. Being able to skip the verbal interaction can be a plus, and writing down the question helps me clarify the issues. Getting support online also provides a feeling of participation in the problem-solving process and I sometimes go online even when I know the answer to my problem might be available more quickly (and cheaply) by regular phone call. The chance of learning something new while scanning posted information makes it seem worthwhile.

Online Support at Microsoft

To find out what it's like behind the scenes in online support I talked to Runnoe Connally of Microsoft Corporation. Connally manages the Microsoft Connection, that company's online offering on CompuServe and GEnie, and he spoke with some pride about his experience running one of the most active and innovative of the manufacturers' support forums.

Microsoft offers three online services. Our commercial network is called Microsoft Online. I run the other two on CompuServe and GEnie. CompuServe is by far the largest. We position the Microsoft Connection above phone support but below our commercial developer network,

Online. Developers pay an annual fee to get onto that one. It has consulting services, among other things.

On CompuServe and GEnie, up until we opened the Windows Forum, we logged between 2800 and 3000 messages per week. The Windows Forum by itself has doubled that, so now we're taking 6000 messages per week. The messages are only a small part of it. A lot of the people log on to read messages or download files without actually leaving a message. Some people log on several times a week, but the actual log-ons are over 100,000 a month. It's very significant.

I asked Connally if he had any idea how many tech support calls he heads off by way of this service. He acknowledged that it's a little hard to judge.

We usually figure, by a rough rule of thumb, that one message on CompuServe probably takes care of from five to 10 people, judging from the number of log-ons and file downloads. One reason that CompuServe is so efficient is that, unlike on the telephone where you can just help one person at a time, on CompuServe someone will post a question and we'll answer it and maybe a dozen people are helped by that, but hundreds of people will have actually read it. There are a lot of people who are what we call lurkers; they get in and they read the message threads, but they never say anything. When you ask, "How many people have we actually helped?" maybe immediately we've only helped a dozen people, but down the road somebody else who has read it will consciously or unconsciously remember the information was there. They'll be helped without realizing where they got the information.

The other thing we like is not just that the questions and answers get on the message base, but we also have our knowledgebase online, so that common questions or more detailed explanations than you can provide in a short message are available to all of our users. They can go to the knowledgebase, browse, and get all the information about a particular product. So they're getting taken care of even if they never left a message.

Maybe they've got a particular file that just isn't working for whatever reason. You can't upload a file on the telephone, but you can upload it on CompuServe. Sometimes there's a thin line between helping a person and actually doing it for them, but there's so much more that we can do for a person online than we can on the telephone. It's much more efficient. We get more accomplished, the customer's happy, and we're happy.

I broached what I consider a possible disadvantage—that you have to rely on people to give you the information you need. You can't ask them questions interactively. Connally explained how online help addresses this and added that what might at first seem a liability is in fact an asset.

In our forum announcements we specify exactly how thoroughly we want people to explain how their systems are configured—what hardware they have, what software they're running, what TSRs [memory resident software] they have. If they read the announcements, when they first post the question we'll have most of the information we need. If we need more information we'll ask them and they'll post a second message.

On CompuServe everything is in black and white, so it's real clear exactly what the customer said and how you responded to it. On the phone a customer may not give you all the information he thought he did. He'll try something and it doesn't work and he'll come back ticked off and say, "I told you such-and-such," and how can you tell? On CompuServe it's obvious. If he didn't give you all the information, or he gave you incorrect information, there's no argument, it's right there in black and white. I much prefer CompuServe to the phone.

In trying to determine how much time is devoted to a CompuServe question as opposed to a telephone support call,

Connally introduced another consideration—the different levels of customer expertise the two systems attract.

One problem in comparing telephone and online support is that on the telephone a lot of the users are first-time users. They call in for help in installing the program. On CompuServe you don't usually get that kind of low-level question. Simply because they're on an electronic bulletin board, they're somewhat above your occasional user. They're more knowledgeable, more computer literate. They use the equipment more often. So when they do have questions, these tend to be more technical, more difficult, and at least to my staff, they tend to be a little more interesting.

We get a lot more questions that have to be researched, since they are more technical. If we don't have an answer within 24 hours, we'll just respond to the user's message saying, "We're working on it, we'll get back to you."

We talked about staffing. If we restrict the question just to the four Microsoft forums (Connally operates two others for vendors who have products running under Windows), Connally has half a dozen assistant sysops (system operators) working directly under him. Some of them are Microsoft employees, and some of them are independent. The people who actually answer the technical questions are called section leaders. They number 15 working in seven different product groups. Connally also has several people doing customer service, one person for U.S. customers, one for Canadian, and one for everybody else.

In addition to the section leaders and the assistant sysops, Connally has two other categories of people—Microsoft volunteers and technical assistants. The volunteers are not actually in customer support. They're from other parts of the company and they like talking to customers. They log on whenever they feel like it and answer questions. Technical assistants, or TAs, are volunteers from outside the company. Getting on and answering questions is a form of advertising for some of these people. All totalled, there are probably around 40 people that work for

Connally doing online support, though they're not all in his department or even employed by Microsoft.

Some of Connally's section leaders also do phone support, but because of the technical nature of CompuServe, they have to have been on phone support anywhere up to a year before they're allowed online.

> When someone comes into product support they get trained, and then they get on the phones under close supervision. After they've been on the phones for quite some time and they're familiar with the product and with talking with customers, then they're allowed on CompuServe. Because of its high visibility we've got to have the best. Not only technically the best, but also the best customer relations skills. It's usually considered a bit of a plum to work on CompuServe. It is fun in many ways. I'll only take the best and brightest.

Connally's remarks suggested that CompuServe is considered a high profile way for Microsoft to market itself.

> In the last year there's been a real awareness in the rest of the company of CompuServe's impact. We started off just doing technical support, but I've always felt CompuServe could do more than support. There is PR potential there also.
>
> We've got 40 or 50 managers in other departments—in development, applications, systems, marketing, or wherever, who like to get on CompuServe. Some of them just want to listen to what customers are talking about—what problems they're having, what features they'd like to have in the future.
>
> Other managers actually like to get on and interact with the customers. Customers' comments are getting copied and passed around in Microsoft. Whether or not they realize it, every single comment is probably passed around to half a dozen departments. Our customers are really having an effect on the direction of Microsoft products.

Given that Connally feels CompuServe users are more technically astute, I asked him whether they were an especially influential segment of Microsoft's customers.

> I would say so. For the telephone support calls we keep a record of problems customers are having for a number of reasons, particular problems with particular products. If there is a problem with a product we become aware of it fairly quickly. It goes into a database and it's passed on to development.
>
> With CompuServe a lot of the managers bypass that database and go right to the customers, getting into long threads with people talking about their products. The customers get taken care of, because the managers really know the product inside and out. The managers get valuable feedback. These customers, whether they realize it or not, are talking with the guy that helped write the product, and that's got to have an effect.

Microsoft's knowledgebases on CompuServe and GEnie work much the way one presumes they would. Phone support people keep a record of their questions and answers. If the question seems useful, it gets filtered into the knowledgebase. When somebody calls up and asks a question that a particular phone tech hasn't heard before, the tech person can quickly scan the knowledgebase. If it's not there he can always escalate it to a support engineer or whomever. Eventually that problem and solution too will be added to their constantly growing knowledgebase of problems and solutions relating to all of their products in different environments.

The knowledgebase is available to everybody at Microsoft. As Connally says, "There's too much out there for anyone to know everything about any one thing." It is the same knowledgebase they have made available on CompuServe and GEnie, so that any customer can go through the threads and find the answer to his problem.

If there is a longer file that is the solution for a particular problem, you can download it. You may need a Hewlett-Packard driver, for example. It's the same file that Microsoft would mail to you if you were to call up and ask for it. If you want, you can call, wait a week, and get it in the mail, or you can log onto CompuServe and download it immediately—templates, macros, drivers, patches, applications notes, maybe a dozen different types of files. All this is available because, as Connally says, "The more we take care of the customer, the more likely he is to come back to us the next time he needs help, or another product for that matter."

I asked Connally what it's like managing the online services— whether it is a relatively smooth process.

It can be fun and it can be extremely frustrating at the same time. Nothing really quite prepared me for this job. Up until September of '87 there was no official support for Microsoft products on CompuServe. There were a lot of users helping other users and a bunch of volunteers, but there was nothing organized. There's a tremendous amount of work involved.

I'll give you a short example, something you don't usually think about. A lot of the programs available on CompuServe are written by users. It could be shareware or public domain stuff. When they upload a file we have to check it out. When the file goes up it goes into a preview buffer and nobody but a sysop can see it. We have to make sure that we had a good upload, it wasn't a corrupted file, and that there's no line noise that ruined it. That doesn't happen very often but it does happen.

Assuming it's okay, we have to make sure there are no viruses in it. There have been a lot of virus scares in the industry but to my knowledge, I've only heard about one virus on CompuServe, and that was a year or two ago. It was caught before any users found it. As far as I know, no user has ever gotten an infected program from CompuServe from any company. The sysops on all of the forums on CompuServe (there are about 500), take it really seriously. We do everything we can do to check out files, which is why when you upload a file you're not going to see it show up the next day. There's going to be a lag time of several days to a week.

We don't check just for viruses. We also make sure that the program actually works, that it's not so buggy it's going to crash your system. If there's a major problem, we get back to the author and say, "This has to be fixed before we'll make it available." Minor bugs we're not going to worry about too much—nothing's perfect. But does it in general do what the file description says it's going to do?

Within reason we try to make sure that nobody uploaded a copyrighted program or plagiarized somebody else's work. In Windows we're getting a lot of files uploaded that are images of one kind or another. One guy uploaded a picture of Calvin and Hobbs. That's copyrighted, so it's not going to be made available to the public. Another individual uploaded a picture of a seminaked lady in handcuffs. That's not exactly appropriate, so I didn't make that available. We don't really ask ourselves if the file is useful or not. We let the users decide that. There's a lot of behind the scenes work that our users never imagine.

Connally's closing remarks evaluated the efficiency of CompuServe system administration and the ease of use of its interface.

I can think of numerous improvements to the system that I would like to see, and I've sent CompuServe a wish list. CompuServe is constantly evaluating a lot of things. It's easy for me to see additional features, but I'm not on the programming end of CompuServe.

The ease of use of CompuServe user interface depends to a great extent on the communications software you get. CompuServe recently came out with something called the CompuServe Information Manager, or CIM for short, which is a Windows-like interface. It doesn't actually run under Microsoft Windows, which I wish it did. CompuServe has been making an effort to make things more user-friendly. It is still not easy as it could be, but I have seen improvement.

Technical Knowledgebases

Every manufacturing company creates mountains of technical information about its products, and most of it has been unavailable to users unless they called for support and knew the right question to ask. Documentation supplied with products can, at best, encompass only the most widely useful of this information, but there are times when users, especially expert users, field technicians, and consultants, need access to the arcane technical details that rarely find a place in the manual.

Manufacturers, resellers, and third-party information providers have begun to realize that making this kind of technical documentation available to the users makes sound economic sense. Whether they sell the information or give it away, they're using computer technology like CD-ROM and magnetic media to publish and distribute technical bulletins, specifications, diagrams, and compatibility data, thereby easing their own support burden and making their users more self-sufficient.

Providing technical information by electronic means has several advantages over printed media. Cost is obviously a factor. After spending a few thousand dollars producing a master, a company can produce a CD-ROM disk for a couple of dollars, and the disk can contain 600 megabytes of information. Floppy disks are even cheaper when the size of the knowledgebase is smaller. Ease of updating information is another factor. Not least, electronic knowledgebases enable users to find the data they need with sophisticated search software, then print out paper copies if and when needed.

TECHS—Building a Single Source for Technical Information

I talked to Jeff Schwartz of TECHS International, an Anaheim, California-based company that repackages technical information from a large number of hardware and software manufacturers. Schwartz did field support for six years installing PCs and LANs before starting TECHS International. He kept having an experience that most technicians will recognize. He'd be working late and find himself needing to know some minor technical fact like a switch setting and suddenly realize he was dead in the water—he couldn't get through to the relevant manufacturer because the support staff was gone for the day. "It's ridiculous," he thought, "we can't get this information when we need it. There should be an industry clearinghouse for this stuff."

There wasn't, so a year and a half ago he started one. His wife came up with the name, which stands for Technical Encyclopedia of Computer Hardware and Software. The idea is simple: manufacturers provide their technical information—bulletins, specs, diagrams, whatever—to TECHS International, which then culls it, indexes it, and puts it on disks. The product subscribers receive—also called TECHS—includes a proprietary search engine, an initial compilation of information on floppy disks, and monthly updates incorporating new data. When I spoke to Schwartz, TECHS had about 34 megabytes of information and was growing at the rate of three or four megabytes a month.

There's much more data that could be added, perhaps 20 to 25 megabytes a month. But the stumbling block is the time-consuming preprocessing required before the data is searchable with the TECHS search engine. The user would look first for a subject category, then a manufacturer, and then search for specifics. Human editors have had to structure the information and create pointers and cross references, a very labor intensive process. TECHS is on the verge of changing to a new approach whereby data is searched by key words, and this should greatly reduce the amount of labor needed to get new material into the knowledgebase. Schwartz feels that at some point TECHS's growth will level off, but not before it reaches several hundred megabytes.

Although CD-ROM may eventually be the way TECHS International distributes its knowledgebase, floppy disks are the present medium. Not enough people have CD-ROM drives, and magnetic disks are presently easier to use in conjunction with network technology.

The emphasis has been mostly on hardware—PCs and "anything that attaches to them." But software manufacturers like Lotus and Novell are also joining up. Manufacturers have provided their informational raw material for free. Some would have been happy to pay to have someone make the stuff available. They agree not to make their technical information available through any other company. When I talked to Jeff, over 90 different companies were signed on and another one or two were being added every month. They find having their information available on TECHS eases their support burden and enhances the perception of their products. Soon there will be a TECHS logo sticker for the packages of supported products.

Subscribers pay in the neighborhood of $100 a month for a single user version of TECHS and about twice that for the network version. Subscriptions bring monthly updates and any changes to the search engine. Subscribers can add their own information to the system, and there is nothing in the technology that limits it to computer information. Graphics are supported.

The search software was designed for ease of use. Users can negotiate it with only a couple of keys. Schwartz looked at some of the other information storage and retrieval products on the market but found them too complicated. "This isn't a product you use when you're happy. The last thing you want when you're in trouble is something that makes your life more difficult."

Fax Support

The ubiquitous fax machine isn't glamorous technology. The

output isn't pretty and it doesn't transmit machine-readable data like e-mail or other online media. But unlike telecommunication it's easy and it's finding plenty of uses. There are over three million fax machines in use in the United States, and if you have access to one you can order sandwiches with it or advertise your business, and now you can use it to get help with your computer.

Most technical support departments have fax machines and many are finding them invaluable to aid standard telephone support. Users can fax in examples of bad output, and the support staff can fax back technical bulletins, diagrams, or simply get an answer to a caller who's hard to reach by phone. Some support departments are beginning to encourage their customers to fax in questions instead of calling.

New fax technology has been developing that makes this medium much more powerful than simple send and receive units. Networked servers allow companies to automatically respond to special fax inquiry forms or to touchtone signals punched in on users' telephones. Intel Corporation's FaxBack support service, for example, allows users to punch phone keys to request that an extensive list of technical bulletins be faxed to them. If they think one of the bulletins will fill their needs, they can request it, again using their touchtone phone, and it will be faxed to them immediately. You can also fax written questions to Intel and receive a written reply the same way.

Intel receives an average of 15 to 25 fax messages per day, and generates an equivalent number of responses. They advertised their service by publishing the 800 number for sending faxes in their manuals and sales literature. As they make presentations to dealers, user groups, and customers, they make a point of mentioning it.

Intel Corporation's Al Kinney provided answers to my questions about his company's use of fax for support. He began by describing the kind of fax technology they use and the kinds of questions that lend themselves to fax versus phone handling.

We use our Intel Connection CoProcessor Fax boards, installed in standard AT-type systems. We're currently using two systems, each with a CCP installed, but will later be putting multiple boards in a single system, as volumes demand it.

Basically fax questions parallel the type of questions we hear on the telephone lines. The biggest difference is that fax questions sometimes have more information and are better organized than the questions we receive on the telephone. We tend to answer them more efficiently. In general, too, fax allows us more time to explore a complex problem and provide the answer the first time we contact the customer. If we receive a phone call with a complex problem, many times it results in two or three return calls to get information and get an answer for the question.

It's not really effective to compare fax versus online versus phone calls. Each serves a segment of the customer base, and they augment rather than replace each other. However, we are encouraging customers to contact us via fax or online, rather than the telephone. Because there is an expectation of a response within a day or two, it's less "pressure" to handle customer inquiries via fax or online than on the phone.

Voice Response Systems

Anyone who's had to answer endless repetitive support questions must have been struck by the waste of time and brain power required to parrot back the same old answers day after day. Though the problem may be fresh and important to the caller, the support person is likely to feel poorly used. Worse, while the routine questions are being answered, other callers, perhaps with more challenging problems, are kept on hold or get a busy signal. One approach to the problem is to maintain different levels of staffing, with less expert techs on the front lines, ready to handle routine calls and more experienced ones available for the stumpers. But this approach may simply beg the question, "Is any support person going to be happy for long when most of his work is repetitive?"

Phones that Answer Themselves

Can technology help deal with this problem? If we can call our banks and get our account balances and find out if our checks have cleared, why can't we use smart telephone technology to handle some of these routine questions?

Support managers have begun experimenting with ways to use their automatic call distributors, ACDs, to deliver frequently requested information. Ashton-Tate has created a system called Auto-Tate that delivers answers to frequently asked questions about its Multimate word processors. The trouble is that ACDs just aren't designed to allow complex interactions between caller and information that would allow the system to actually help diagnose and solve problems.

One company, Intellisystems of Chatsworth, California, has developed a specialized support product called TechSys that weds expert systems and digitized voice technology to deliver solutions. Callers hear the digitized voice of a support rep who explains the mechanics of the system and then asks the caller to hit keys on his touch tone phone in response to questions about the computer configuration and symptoms.

A diagnostic dialogue ensues, just as in any expert system, with the caller's responses leading, hopefully, to the right solution. If the system doesn't yet have the answer to the caller's problem, he can be transferred to a live support person or asked to call back when one is available. One nice touch is that the caller can bail out of the session at any time to try a solution, get a call number from the system, then call back if necessary to resume where he left off.

TechSys produces reports of callers' sessions, allowing management to pinpoint common problems and places where the system's expertise needs to be improved. Modifying the system's knowledgebase is said to be a relatively simple process within the abilities of a support staff. Staff can also tap into the expert system for training or troubleshooting sessions.

Intellisystems claims it's system can handle 20 percent to 50 percent of common support questions, the low-level ones that don't require any fresh thinking. A typical session might be three to four minutes on the phones and about six responses from the caller. About fifteen of the systems are in use in support centers, including one of the biggest, Microsoft, where TechSys is being used to answer questions about the Flight Simulator software during the product's busy season.

The obvious objection to a system like TechSys is that callers in trouble want to talk to people, not machines, and that companies

will lose touch with their customers. Intellisystems replies that its systems can be available when human tech reps aren't—at night or on weekends, for example—or when hold times for human support are long. Callers are likely to be pleased rather than angry to have the option. It says one of its customers has surveyed callers and found that over 87 percent would use the system again.

TechSys is not simple technology and it's not cheap. Its custom hardware incorporates two 386 processors running in parallel in the protected mode. Systems are custom configured and can handle up to 60 incoming lines. Prices start in the mid $30,000 range and an average system is about $60,000, including 20 hours of customization for the buyer's product line. If the system can deliver on its promise to handle a significant part of the support burden, or make customers happy when they call after hours, it wouldn't take long to pay for itself. Deciding how to use the technology effectively and sensitively will be an interesting management challenge.

Remote Control Software

Anyone who's ever done telephone technical support knows the frustration of not being able to see what's going on on the caller's system. Using the mind's eye and the clumsy tools of spoken language, a skillful support person can usually figure out what's happening—eventually. But wouldn't it be great to be able to reach out and "touch" the user's system, get the information that's needed, and maybe even fix the problem.

Remote control software fulfills this tech support fantasy. Numerous commercial software packages make it possible for two computers to be linked by modem and telephone line so that a support specialist can see what the user is doing, look into the files on the remote system, even transmit and install software patches.

Most vendors' tech support operations would have difficulty implementing this kind of remote access. Both the customer and the support center have to be equipped with modems and matching support software costing up to a couple of hundred dollars, luxuries that would be unthinkable for handling routine support calls. But when vendors sell the kind of support contracts that provide for extensive consultation, remote control support becomes an option. Inhouse support centers could also find ways to use remote computing to help far-flung users, combining support functions with remote training capabilities.

Tech III is a third-party support company specializing in database programming and support that has enthusiastically adopted remote control software to help it's customers. Located in Los Angeles with a staff of six programmers, a dedicated support person, and a testing person, Tech III has used both Close-Up (Norton-Lambert Corp.) and Carbon Copy Plus (Microcom Software), depending on what its customers have. I talked to Richard Grossman of Tech III about how his company has used this technology.

We've been doing remote support since '86, because that's when the traffic in L.A. started getting really bad. It was actually better during the Olympics than it was after, so to avoid going onsite we started doing more phone support. I started to slant my rates so it would be more expensive to make an onsite call. We have a two-hour minimum onsite, but we have a twelve minute minimum on the phone. We did that to encourage people to use the phone support, especially if it's something short.

You get really tired of dictating commands and asking people what it says. The other thing is we also can fix bugs and deliver updates right over the phone. We do that a lot. When a project is really happening, we might be sending updates every day or every couple of days by modem.

Although the advertised concept is that you could see a bug happening online, it's only rarely that we actually need to do that. Usually what will happen is the customer will tell us about a problem and we'll run the application on our system and we'll see the problem, since we already have it here. But sometimes it's data-related. It's a problem that won't happen with test data.

The number one thing we use it for is just taking over DOS, moving things around in the customer's system, and seeing what's in the CONFIG.SYS and AUTOEXEC. We make sure all the files are there, and upload new fix files. We reindex and then test the program again on the customer's side. Every once in a while, we'll run a report for somebody overnight, because both Close-Up and Carbon Copy allow you to dial in and disconnect without rebooting. If you want to, you can dial in again, echo to your printer, and see what a report is up to—see how it's progressing.

Some of our programmers have two computers, so we can keep working on one while we're doing something on the other system. With one of them I'll do remote support, and I'll use Close-Up or Carbon Copy, and if it's sitting there reindexing the files I can keep working with my other system.

We almost always use external modems because of the diagnostics you get from the lights. I've found that even users who don't know anything about anything will notice if a light isn't flashing. External modems are also easier to switch if there's a problem.

Right now we're using 2400 baud modems. We'd like to be using 9600, but there's no point in us getting 9600 if we can't get the customers to get 9600, and almost nobody has any interest whatsoever in spending a thousand dollars on a modem. If 9600s can get down to $350 to $550, it'll start being practical.

In terms of speeds, I consider 1200 baud unusable. I consider 2400 excruciating. It's not fun supporting at 2400 baud, but it's less painful than dictating commands over the telephone. If 9600 catches on, or if the whole country goes to ISDN so that you don't even need a modem, that'll be really exciting, because then you can plug into some system and it'll be reasonably quick. Now, if you make a mistake while you're supporting somebody, it takes forever to do it again. While the machine's updating, you can't zip around like you can on your own machine. So, 2400 baud has some limitations.

I would never live without remote control. Some things are just too technical to be asking the user. The alternative is going there.

Support by Wire

So far, no one has come up with a substitute for a smart, helpful human being when someone needs help with a computer problem. The technologies we've looked at here all have something to offer to the support process, but they're still just tools to help people help people. Someday, software and hardware may be a lot better at diagnosing their own problems and communicating directly with support providers when needed. Until then, it's nice to have some power tools handy to help deliver answers.

A User's Guide to Tech Support

Most computer users can tell horror stories about their experiences trying to get help with computer problems. Constant busy signals, hours on hold, incompetent support reps giving incorrect information or shuffling callers off to someone else's support line. All these complaints and more are commonplace. Though much of the unhappiness stems from the uneven quality and increasing cost of support, a good deal comes from not knowing who to call, how to get through to and work effectively with support staff, and how to influence manufacturers to improve their products and service. This chapter focuses on techniques users can employ to get the help they need quickly and efficiently.

Why a chapter devoted to how to *get* better support in a book directed towards people who *give* it? First off, like all other computer users, you're going to need help sooner or later with a product you *don't* know like the back of your hand, so you might as well learn to be an expert help receiver. Second and more important, this chapter is intended to get you thinking about support from the user's point of view so you can give better service in the long run.

Use these tips for users as a stimulus to thinking about your own organization and how the people you support can get the best possible help from it. Think about how you would like users to behave when they need your help and about ways you might encourage them in that direction. Think, too, about the obstacles users experience when they contact you and how they should best negotiate those obstacles. Then tell the users.

How Important Is Support to You?

Since you're reading this book, computer technical support is important to you, but that may not mean that support is a crucial issue when making every purchase decision. Technical support is more important when you or your company face the following scenarios.

- You depend on the product for your business or other important purpose.

- You plan to use the product for a long time.

- You have many people using it, especially novice or unsophisticated users.

- You spend a lot of time with the product.

- You work in a complex technical environment, or need to adapt the product to a new use.

- You don't have other sources of support like an inhouse help desk.

  Or when the product is

- Complex

- Expensive (you'd better get your money's worth)

- Subject to breakdown (hardware)

- Rapidly evolving

Support may be less than crucial if the product is for recreational or occasional use, if it's used by experts who can decipher obscure documentation and solve most of their own problems, or if it's relatively simple. Remember, though, that the simplest software or hardware will cause problems and the best documentation will have gaps.

Before You Buy

After you've bought the hardware or software it's already too late to exercise your primary power to influence the quality of the vendor's support. That power comes from voting with your wallet for the manufacturers and dealers who offer quality support. Before you make any purchasing decision about products you will depend on, ask some pointed questions such as those below of the dealer or vendor.

- Is free support available? Does the vendor expect the user to get support from a dealer instead of directly?

- If there's free support from the vendor, how long does it last?

- Is this an absolute cutoff, or are users allowed to get help for defects and bugs after free support is over?

- What hours is support available?

- Are there toll charges?

- How hard is it to get through on support lines?

- Are support lines staffed by knowledgeable people?

- Are there extended service contracts available and, if so, how much do they cost? Are there different levels of support depending on how much you pay?

Other aspects of support. These questions focus on telephone support, but there's more to support than hotlines. Buyers should investigate other aspects of a vendor's total customer service program before making purchase decisions.

- What warranties are provided?

- Is there a money-back policy if the product doesn't meet your needs? For how long?

- Does the vendor supply informational materials such as newsletters to registered users?

- Is there a computer bulletin board or user forum sponsored by the manufacturer?

- For software, how often is the product upgraded and what are the charges for upgrading? Does the vendor inform registered owners of upgrades or significant bugs?

- For hardware, how readily available are service centers, spare parts, and other supplies? Is the vendor prepared to carry replacement parts indefinitely? Is onsite service available? Remember, all hardware breaks sooner or later!

How Do You Find Out?

If you're convinced that you need to evaluate support along with other factors of product quality, you may have to do some digging. Let's discuss some of the chief sources of information.

Product Reviews The computer press has increasingly been including assessments of support policies in reviews of products, though the practice is far from universal. Some reviewers recount their experiences dealing with hotlines in some detail, providing a sense of what you might expect. Others include a brief, cursory description of the vendor's policy and whether a sample question was answered satisfactorily. Generally, a good review should include a description of support *policies* as well as *performance*, how well the vendor executes those policies. It's a shame that most reviews don't cover other aspects of customer support beyond telephone support lines, like service availability or upgrade and return policies.

You should bear in mind that reviewers routinely base their assessments on one or two encounters with a technical support line, and may generalize unfairly, reaching conclusions from those encounters that are either too positive or too negative. Everyone, even the best tech support person, has an off day. Remember, too, that as computer experts most reviewers may not ask the kinds of questions less experienced users ask. And sometimes reviewers get a different kind of support than normal callers. They may be given special numbers to call or be issued evaluation copies with special serial numbers. Though reviewers usually try to give the hotline a fair test, they may not be able to remain incognito.

Word of Mouth Talking to present users of the product you're considering, or users of other products by the same company, will give you some of the best information about what to expect in the way of service and support. Naturally, it's important to determine how much experience your informant has had with the company and when. Larger companies may have developed a reputation for good or bad support that's so widespread that even noncustomers will confidently give you a report card. You might be better off ignoring this kind of rep, or at least checking it against other sources. Companies change, for better or for worse, sometimes faster than their reputations.

Many computer products are made by small companies, the kind that don't have widespread name recognition beyond their narrow market area and therefore don't have wide-spread reputations. Some producers of specialized (and expensive) products may have less than a dozen clients. Often these vendors can supply lists of their customers and it's wise to call a few to get the benefit of their experience.

. . . .

Your Own Investigation

Getting a true picture of the level of support you're going to get will ultimately depend on doing your homework. Read the software package, and if possible, the documentation for descriptions of support policies and phone numbers. Some companies seem to go out of their way to hide the phone numbers for support lines, as if that would discourage callers. That's a bad sign, though hardly conclusively damning. Increasingly, vendors proudly proclaim the level of support on all their literature and even packing materials. Talk to the dealer of the product about whether he has had dealings with the company's support lines.

Then call the company. Many have separate phone numbers for corporate business, customer service, and technical support. Customer service is generally concerned with nontechnical services. These folks are usually not trained to provide very technical information or do troubleshooting; they will generally refer callers with technical questions to the tech support lines. It's worthwhile to call customer service as well as technical support, though, because you will depend on both during your ongoing relationship with the vendor. Ask customer service to describe the vendor's policy on technical support, including the kinds of questions listed above. Then ask if they can send you literature, supply product specifications or warranty information, tell you if an upgrade is expected soon, or, for hardware, tell you where your nearest service facility is. Do they seem knowledgeable and helpful? Don't expect them to be technical experts, but you do want assurance that they can supply the more general information you'll need.

Then try the tech support hotline. You might have trouble getting through at all. Clogged phone lines are a fact of life at many vendors. Try a half-dozen times at different times of day and if that doesn't work, take it as a bad omen. You may also be stymied by the vendor's eligibility screening. Perhaps only registered owners can get past the telephone system by way of a special code. Whether such obstacles constitute a strike against the vendor is something you must decide. If you have trouble, you might call customer service back, saying you're a prospective buyer with a technical question and ask if they can put you through to technical support. It should be possible for a serious prospective customer to talk to the hotline about a presales technical question, such as how the product can be expected to work with some other product you use. If and when you get through, try to assess the support person's technical knowledge, communications skills, and patience. Do they give the impression of working within a well-managed organization? Do they have information close at hand? Do they have a strong service orientation?

Get the Total Picture

Throughout the computer industry the service orientation of vendors varies dramatically. Some companies tend to say yes to the customer whenever possible, whether it's a question of offering high-quality telephone support or, perhaps, bending a return policy in favor of the customer. Others seem to put up obstacles, to scrimp, to offer minimal service, to fail to listen, to say no. Some of these latter vendors are shoestring operations on the edge of survival, but others have leading positions in their markets, perhaps able to prosper because of technical quality or early entry in the field. Dominance may lead to arrogance and arrogance generally leads to poor support. Making a purchase decision against a market-dominant vendor that offers poor support may take some courage, but may save you a lot of grief in the long run.

How you weigh the importance of support against other qualities like price, features, and performance is up to you, but I would emphasize one point. Developing and maintaining an effective technical support operation is a difficult, often unsung achievement, and a company that succeeds with technical support is likely to be around for the long haul.

After You Buy but Before You Call

Though I've just spent several pages talking about the importance of support and how to assess support quality before you buy, I want to dwell a little now on why you don't want to call that technical support line right away at the first sign of trouble, what you should try to do to solve your own problems, and how to prepare for the call when it becomes necessary.

You don't want to call at the drop of a hat because, first of all, calling for help is time consuming. Finding the number, dialing, redialing if busy, and waiting for an actual human being to answer are bound to take a while, even before you start counting the time spent describing the problem and, hopefully, getting a solution.

If most callers spent that same amount of time reading their documentation and rethinking what they're doing, there would be a drastic reduction in the demand for support. Many callers seem so intimidated by their manuals that they're afraid to open them. Whoever's to blame for that, a post-literate society or incompetent documentation writers, it's clear that these people don't get the benefits from their systems that they might because they don't know what's there. Some estimates put the amount of functionality users are getting from their computer products at 20 percent. By struggling a little with the manual and the system you gain considerable power as you gain self-sufficiency. You're almost certain to learn more from solving a problem yourself than just the answer to the problem itself.

There's clearly a time when struggling further with a problem is counterproductive. Frustration, time taken from other work, and equipment downtime all have to be considered when deciding when to call. Experienced users develop a sense of when their own efforts are unlikely to succeed, or when there's a piece of the puzzle that just isn't available in the documentation. Here are some things to check before you call.

Rethink what you're doing. Pausing and rethinking the procedure you're attempting is the best and fastest way to solve computer problems. Pay close attention and go through the steps slowly and deliberately, pausing often to observe what's happening. A very high percentage of trouble calls are caused by simple user errors, so be a little suspicious of yourself. It can help to talk things through with someone, even if they're not particularly expert.

Is the answer in the documentation? If you're reading this you're probably the type who at least tries to consult the manual before calling for help, even after repeated frustration with the quality of documentation. Just where to look is often unclear. Check the index, the table of contents, the reference section, any tutorials covering the problem area, and, of course, the trouble-shooting section if there is one. Don't forget the parts of the documentation that come on software release disks. Readme files often provide the solutions to the most annoying problems because the problems hadn't been encountered yet when the manual was written. Indexes in computer documentation can be atrocious (even nonexistent), so you may have to be imaginative to find the answer. Try any possible synonyms for the subject you're working on. Sometimes you find the place in the manual where the subject is covered but the language is so vague that it's nearly useless. In this case you probably need to call. Make sure you complain about the manual!

Check the usual suspects. Certain gremlins strike over and over, causing even experienced computer users grief. Even though you're sure there's something wrong with your new software or equipment, it could turn out there's just a loose cable, wrong port name, syntax error, or memory resident program conflict to blame for your malfunction. Before assuming that the cause is more esoteric, go over the fundamentals as thoroughly as possible, making sure that you've followed the basic installation and configuration instructions and that your hardware is connected properly.

Try the vanilla test. It's much harder to diagnose a problem on a complicated system than a simple one, and many problems are caused by compatibility problems. Reduce the system to the simplest configuration that supports the process you're trying to get working. This might mean booting the computer from a floppy, or removing special devices from the configuration. Go back to basics first, see if you can get that working, then add other software and hardware to the stew one piece at a time, confirming at each point that the system is still working correctly. For a more detailed discussion, see Chapter 4, *Handling Support Calls*.

Just where is the problem? Whether you try to solve your own problem or call immediately for help, your hardest task may be to figure out just where the problem is. Doing the vanilla test as described above will simplify matters, but still you may be left unclear about what part of the system is to blame. Try to devise simple tests that eliminate one part of the system after another until you can be sure which subsystem is acting up. Use any resources you have such as spare hardware that allow you to "swap out" one possibly faulty component for one that you know works.

Can you repeat it? Fundamental to solving a problem is figuring out exactly when it happens—what conditions are necessary to cause the problem to occur. Make careful observations about which steps lead to the problem and under which conditions. Take clear notes. Some problems may be intermittent, but with a little care you might be able to discover patterns to the system behavior that point to the cause.

Is it really supposed to do what you want? Many hotline callers suffer extended frustration with products because they want the hardware or software to do something that it's just not designed to do. After a lot of struggle they have nothing to show for their efforts. Take a moment when you're stuck to confirm that the system is supposed to do what you want. Of course, you may have to call a help line just to get the definitive answer. Most vendors avoid making clear declarations in their documentation and marketing materials about the limitations of their products, which may make for a few more sales but ultimately leads to more support calls and customer frustration.

When You're Stuck, Be Prepared

You've given it your best shot but you're stuck. You need information or troubleshooting help from someone who knows the product intimately. You've done your best to figure out just what piece of software or equipment is causing you grief and your first impulse is to call up the vendor and demand that they help you out of your jam—after all, they put you there! It's reasonable to expect that you as the consumer should be able to expect help when you have difficulty with a product. Unfortunately, the reality is that no law guarantees your right to support (though legislators are working on that). The availability and quality of tech support varies tremendously across the computer industry, from free, toll-free, and high-quality support to nonexistent, which is why I emphasized the wisdom of buying with support quality in mind. Now, when you need help is not the best time to discover that support requires an expensive subscription or is not available at all. Luckily, most companies in the industry do provide some kind of telephone help line. By being prepared you can maximize the service you can get from them.

Before you pick up the phone there are a number of things you want to do to be ready. If you're prepared you'll get back to work sooner, have a more pleasant time, and increase your chances of getting the right answer the first time. If you're paying for support, or just for the toll charges, you'll save yourself money, and you'll start out by impressing the support person as a competent, savvy computer user, which will probably get you better service.

Know who to call. When you get a new product, assume that sooner or later you'll need to call for help. Make note of the support phone number in the documentation if it's not there already, or keep a binder near the equipment with support phone numbers and notes of contacts with help lines. And remember, not every question will need a technical support line. Many matters can be handled by other, less technically oriented (and less overburdened) customer support or sales lines. Keep these phone numbers handy for help in finding supplies, ordering upgrades, or getting literature on new products.

Protect your eligibility for support. When you buy a product, the support policy of the manufacturer should be spelled out in the supplied documentation, including any limitations on the length of eligibility and any fee arrangements for extended or premium support. Don't ignore this information until you're desperate for help. If you're entitled to free support for, say, 90 days, you should do your best to "shake down" the product as thoroughly as possible within that time. Feel free to call as often as necessary during the free support period to make yourself confident that it can perform properly for your purposes.

If any registration forms are included with the product, make sure you fill them out and send them in. Filing such forms may or may not be necessary to validate your warranty and entitle you to tech support. It does register your ownership and provide a way for the manufacturer to keep you informed of upgrades, bugs, or new products. A certain amount of junk mail may result from sending in these forms, but the benefits are worthwhile.

If the product came with a serial number or support eligibility number, make sure you keep it safe. You may want to keep the serial number secure to guard against unauthorized use (especially important when you're paying for support), but it should be handy enough that authorized users of the product can find it whenever necessary.

Be prepared to tell your story. Before you dial the hotline number you want to have key facts at hand. First of all, you need to be able to give a short description of the problem you're having (or your question). Presenting a concise description at the outset makes a big difference in the efficiency of the call. Don't worry if you don't know the technical terms, just formulate as clear and simple a description as possible in your mind or on paper. Tell the support person what you're trying to do and what happens. This short description may be all the support person needs to hear to come to a conclusion. Generally, a limited number of problems constitutes a large proportion of the calls, so you may be lucky and get an immediate solution to your problem if you give a short, clear description of the problem.

If you don't, the support person will launch into an interrogation designed to elicit clarifying information. You may not be able to anticipate all the questions you'll be asked, but it's likely you'll need to give basic information about your hardware and software configuration. Have the following facts on hand.

- The name of the product you're calling about and its version or model number

- The make and model number of your computer system

- The kind of graphics interface and monitor in the system

- Any special hardware equipment that's used in conjunction with the system (don't talk for a half hour without mentioning that you're on a network)

- The operating system and its version number

- Any software you're using in conjunction with the product you're calling about and the version numbers

If you're calling about a problem, you should collect as much documentation as possible about it. If an error message appears, try to do a screen dump or copy down the exact wording. If there's printed evidence of the problem, have it ready when you call. Whenever a problem is complicated or has an extended history, it's invaluable to keep notes about when it occurs and everything that's been tried to solve it.

One very important aspect of preparation needs to be stressed. When calling with a computer problem, always try to call from the computer site. You'll often need to describe system behavior in detail and to try different things suggested by the support person, and there's no substitute for being able to work with the computer while talking. It's worth going to some effort to get a telephone near the computer, even if this means buying an extra long extension cord or commandeering a cordless phone. Think of a telephone as a basic part of a complete computer workstation. If you're calling in behalf of another user, it's worth a fair amount of inconvenience to be at that person's computer and with them present.

Getting Through

Sometimes the hardest thing about tech support is just getting through to someone. Repeated busy signals and interminable waits on hold while being forced to listen to someone's idea of soothing music (or advertisements for the company's products) are among users' most frequent complaints. Sometimes the fault lies with stingy companies that won't cough up the money necessary to hire and train enough support people and install more phone lines. But the fact is that hotlines are forced to deal with a very uneven demand on their services, so that even the most generous support budget cannot supply enough service to meet peak demand with the same response available during nonpeak hours. If they were to staff for the peaks, their excess capacity during nonpeak hours would constitute a terrible drain on resources. The best that support providers can do is try to set a goal for acceptable service at peak hours and manage their resources to meet it. Whether managers and customers agree on the definition of "acceptable service" is a big question.

Even the best-managed companies are sometimes temporarily overwhelmed by peak demand. That paragon of support, WordPerfect Corporation, found itself drastically unprepared for the volume of calls when it introduced a new release of its word processor, WordPerfect 5.0, and users suddenly found themselves having to dial ten or more times to get through. The company, of course, threw itself into meeting the challenge and got back to normal fairly quickly, and will probably never again underestimate the demands to be expected from a new release.

Consider the alternatives. Struggling with clogged phone lines is no fun, but remember that there may be alternatives. Increasingly, software and hardware companies are offering bulletin boards and other electronic methods of fielding and responding to problems and questions. You can usually post a question and get an answer on a bulletin board within 24 hours, and there's often a library of commonly asked questions that might solve your problem immediately. Even the ubiquitous and easy to use fax machine can be an effective tool for communicating with support departments. You can usually get support fax and bulletin board numbers from companies' corporate switchboards if they're not in the documentation.

Avoid peak hours. Most support lines' peak hours seem to be from 10:00 A.M. until 2:00 P.M. (in their local time). You may not be able to choose the time you call if you're in the middle of something important when disaster strikes, but if there's some flexibility in your work schedule and if you can't get through immediately, it's probably worth waiting for a while.

Interestingly, there seems to be no clear pattern to which days of the week are heavy or light, at least none that different support people agree on. Fridays *may* be a little lighter than other days. Holidays, of course, have a big effect, with volumes usually lower on the days before and after a three-day weekend. In our experience at Computer Hand Holding, call volumes fluctuate fairly widely day to day and week to week following patterns that seem to be pretty random. There is a seasonal pattern that's predictable, though. Volume is considerably lower during the prime vacation months of July and August.

Busy, busy, busy. When faced with hotlines that are so hot they seem to be busy constantly, desperate measures might be in order. A number of software products are on the market that, in conjunction with a modem, are able to dial a number listed on the screen or in a database. These products can usually be set to redial repeatedly until receiving an answer, then notify you with a signal that you've gotten through. Not a bad investment for anyone who does a lot of calling for support, though obviously not of much help if your computer, modem, or the dialing software itself is the subject of the call.

Another approach when desperation sets in is to call other corporate numbers for the company you're trying to reach and impressing the person who answers that you've been trying heroically to get through on the support line. Sometimes a helpful customer service person or receptionist will forward your name and number to the support center with a request for an expedited callback. Don't count on being able to circumvent the normal channels, but it's worth a try.

When you get through, hang on! When your call is answered you may still have to wait awhile before talking to a human being. Increasingly, support centers are using sophisticated (and very expensive) automatic call distributors which answer the phone, greet callers and allow them to direct their call to an appropriate line by hitting a phone key, then place calls in a queue for the next available support person. Simpler devices give a short message and put callers in a single queue. We're all familiar with these systems and they work well enough, but they don't guarantee that your wait for a technician will be a short one. Your best policy, if you have time, is to hang on, unless you're calling during peak hours and decide to try later. Hanging up will mean having to start the process over again, including getting through a possible barrier of busy signals. A speaker phone is a great asset for these long holding patterns.

You may be faced with another substitute for a live human being, phone mail. At Computer Hand Holding, callers who don't get through to human support people within four rings are given the opportunity to leave a message or call back later. About 40 percent don't leave messages, even though we promise to call them back within an hour. This statistic surprises me. I'd have thought people would at least take the opportunity to express their unhappiness (very few do). Perhaps many of these folks simply call back in a few minutes, assuming, rightly, that they have a good chance to get through, or not believing that anyone will call them back if they do leave a message.

We ask callers to leave their names, phone numbers, and the name of the product they're calling about. Some only manage two out of three. Many seem to rush their messages. Make sure you speak c-l-e-a-r-l-y when you leave a message. It's also a good idea to say when you're likely to be available and give an honest assessment of how urgent your problem is.

Hooray, a Human!

Sometimes people are so happy when they reach a live human being who's prepared to help that they treat the support person like a long, lost friend. Others are so aggravated with their problems or the delay in getting through that they blame the tech for everything. Which of these two types is likely to get better service is not difficult to guess. Although it's true that an aggressive, angry customer can sometimes put enough pressure on the support person or his manager to get extraordinary service, it's much more likely to be the friendly, cooperative caller who gets the best help.

Naturally, you want to establish a friendly rapport with the person whose job is to help you. Elsewhere in this book I talk about what the support person should do to establish rapport with the caller and a lot of those tips apply to the caller as well. The basic idea, though, is pretty simple (and old-fashioned). *Treat the support person as you would like to be treated.*

Support people are as varied as any other group, but there are a few generalities about them and their work that I've learned through being one and talking to many of them. When you call for help, bear in mind the following traits that support people usually share.

- In most cases they genuinely like helping people and solving technical problems.

- They spend most of their time dealing with disembodied voices.

- They are often under stress because troubleshooting is mentally taxing, as is adjusting to many different people (who may be under stress themselves).

- They are often further stressed by difficulties getting help themselves when they're stuck.

- They are almost always under pressure to keep calls as short as possible.

- They get tired of dealing with the same old questions by people who haven't bothered to read the manual.

- They are proud of their technical knowledge but may be a little nervous or defensive about what they don't know, which they're confronted with regularly.

- They are rationalists, struggling to make sense of problems (which are chaotic and irrational).

- They don't get a lot of tangible feedback from their work.

Given these generalizations, a few guidelines emerge for getting along well with tech support people.

- At least *try* to find the answer in the documentation before you call.

- Get the person's name and use it to personalize the interaction.

- Make clear you assume the support person is interested in helping you and is trying his best. Don't issue ultimatums or threats.

- Try to reduce stress levels during the call by offering a little small talk or humor, but mostly stay focused on the subject and respect the need to make the call as concise as possible.

- Don't question the support person's competence.

- Try to be as logical and methodical as you can as you collaborate in searching for a solution.

- Share responsibility for finding the answer rather than dumping it in the tech's lap.

- Show some appreciation for the support person's efforts. For outstanding service you might even write a note to the vendor mentioning the name of the person who helped you.

Let's go into a little more detail about how to work with the support staff to get the best, most efficient support possible.

You've got to have a little faith. When you call for help you're a little like a patient visiting a doctor, or a pet owner bringing a dog to a vet. You have to put yourself or your puppy in the hands of an expert and relinquish control to some extent. This means being willing to follow the support person's instructions as they lead you through a troubleshooting procedure without fighting to be in control or to prove that you know more than they do.

This doesn't mean passively relinquishing your common sense or accepting everything the support person says. You have every right to be assertive about the service you deserve, and to make it clear when you don't think you're getting good advice. And there's no contradiction between this point and the suggestion made above that you should share responsibility with the tech for solving your problem. Going limp and expecting that someone else do all the thinking is rarely the right way to deal with a problem. But when callers struggle with support people about how to proceed through the problem-solving process, both parties are likely to lose. The support person will have a frustrating, uphill fight to use the best techniques and the caller will likely spend longer on the phone before getting a solution.

There are times when experienced computer users *are* able to speed things up considerably because they have already done most of the troubleshooting and can focus the call on the key points that they can't answer without consulting tech support. There's obviously no reason to go through the standard procedure when you know just what's needed to solve the problem.

You're their eyes and ears (and fingers). When you call with a problem, support people are completely dependent on you to provide the information about your system. That means you have to leave behind the imprecise language and vague observation most of us use in daily life and get very concrete, accurate, and specific. If you're asked about system behavior, describe it carefully. Instead of saying, "It starts printing way too far to the right," say, "The first character is two and a half inches from the left margin." It's often these details that provide the support person with the key clues to solving the problem.

When the support person asks you to do something on your system, you need to follow his instructions carefully but not mindlessly. Double check the instructions if you have any doubts about what you're being instructed to do. Never rush ahead on the assumption you know what you'll be told to do next. After working with a product for a while, the support person probably knows where you are in the software or what's happening with the equipment, but nobody's perfect, so it's important to keep the support person informed about what you're seeing on the screen as you proceed.

Make haste slowly. Though both you and the support person want to come to a speedy solution, don't rush headlong into a flurry of symptoms and other details. If there are a number of issues you want to discuss, it's usually more effective to deal with them one at a time, taking a step-by-step approach. It may be helpful to start out with an overview of what you want to cover in the call, such as, "I've got a couple of problems…" Sometimes, seemingly discrete symptoms are really linked and a brief description of the separate problems can give the troubleshooter important clues about an underlying cause. But after you've given the overview, you'll get best results by proceeding methodically through the troubleshooting process as led by the support person. One of the hardest kinds of callers for me to deal with is the speed demon, the person who just can't wait to deliver new details, perhaps getting some perverse pleasure from how difficult and complex the problem is. I often need to ask for a slower repeat of the facts. The net effect is a longer call.

Dealing with the Old Runaround

One of the persistent complaints about technical support is that each company is quick to blame others when a problem occurs. Software makers point the finger at hardware, and vice versa. Everyone blames somebody else's product for being poorly behaved. In an industry without many reliable standards, nobody can be compatible with everyone, so there are endless examples of products that just don't work together. At best, software and hardware are only tested with the leading products in each field before release, so there's no assurance what's going to happen when they're used with even slightly less popular products, or even newer (or older) versions of the big-name products. Support centers are limited in how far they can go in trying to recreate an interaction that may be the cause of your problem. They may not have all the software and hardware you're using or the support person may not feel he can take the time to do the necessary testing. It's easy for the tech to assume, rightly or wrongly, that the unfamiliar product is the cause of the problem.

When you're told that the cause of a technical problem is a fault with another product, the support person ought to be able to offer convincing evidence that his supported product is behaving as it's supposed to. That evidence might take the form a demonstration that the product performs properly in isolation, or that it works properly with other hardware or software that you're using. Naturally, the support person has a vested interest in convincing you that the product is functioning properly, and that interest can lead to unconsciously biasing the experiments that supposedly demonstrate that it's working. It's in your interest as a user to judge carefully whether you think the problem does indeed lie elsewhere. On the other hand, you're not doing yourself a favor if you call a tech support line with a hidebound conviction that their product is the culprit when it might be blameless. Some people who don't have a clue about what's causing a problem will convince themselves that it must be caused by company X's product because that's the only support line they can get through to. This practice doesn't do anyone any good.

When the Problem Isn't Solved Immediately

Sometimes the solution to your problem doesn't emerge, even after you and the support person valiantly struggle through the troubleshooting process. You've both tried everything you can think of but your system continues to behave differently than it's supposed to and there's no clear reason why. Or perhaps the support person *can* duplicate the problem, thereby confirming there's a bug. When this occurs, support organizations and the manufacturers they represent really begin to separate themselves between those that follow through and those that give up. Not all problems have solutions, but the best companies have escalation policies that route difficult problems to the second line of support, usually more senior support people, engineers, or technicians whose job it is to take the time to test and troubleshoot the really tough ones.

When a support person tells you that he's going to have to do some research on your problem or refer it to an engineer, you might take some satisfaction in having come up with a real stumper rather than the usual user error or known bug, but you need to do a few things to guarantee that your problem doesn't fall through the cracks.

- Take note of the support person's name. Tactfully make clear that you expect him to take responsibility for following through with your problem, at least to the point of passing it on to the next level of support.

- Ask whether there's a problem number associated with the call and whether the problem is logged into a database. If you have to call back it's useful to know whether the person you subsequently speak with has all the facts.

- Give any phone numbers where you can be reached and a fax number if possible (it's often so hard to reach people that solutions are seriously delayed or even lost).

- Give the support person an honest appraisal of the urgency of the problem. It's probably the best policy not to cry wolf but don't hesitate to make it very clear when a problem has serious consequences.

- Ask when you might expect to hear something back. If the support person can't give you a ballpark estimate of when you might hear something, there's a good chance that you're going to have to call back—perhaps more than once—to check up on the progress of your problem through the troubleshooting process. Call back at reasonable intervals, perhaps weekly, until you get an answer.

Solutions, Temporary and Permanent

The urgency of the problem depends considerably on whether there's a workaround, an alternative way to achieve the basic function for which you use the product. Good support people are trained to find workarounds to help you proceed with your work until the solution is found, but you may have to encourage them. A workaround, though, is supposed to be temporary, not a substitute for the solution of the original problem, unless it gives completely equivalent functionality.

When dealing with software problems, solutions take the form of patches and updates. Patches are fixes to the software code that are designed to solve specific problems and are made available only to users who report those problems. Updates are revisions available to all users. You may be offered a patch that solves your problem immediately, or you might be told that the solution will be available with the next update. When the latter happens, you are, of course, being told to wait for the solution and you should be given an indication of how long that wait will be. The inconvenience, or worse, caused by the delay should never be exacerbated by being told that you will have to pay for the update that solves the problem—if it is, read "When There Is No Solution," below, about how to complain!

When There Is No Solution

It may happen that despite the best efforts of the support staff and their engineering backup your problem has no solution. The software doesn't run properly on your system for unknown reasons or the hardware doesn't meet its specifications, can't be fixed, or won't work in the environment you bought it for. Or the solution to the problem must wait so long for an update that the product loses its value to you. Your choices are limited now. You must decide to either keep the product, with its shortcomings, or try to return it and get your money back.

Warranties and return policies are usually spelled out in fine print in the documentation and almost always limited in time. This is why it's crucial to know about them in advance and to exercise the daylights out of the product during that initial period. Yet it's never possible to be sure that you won't encounter problems after that initial warranty period, sometimes right after. When something goes seriously wrong then, you shouldn't assume that you're out of luck. Many manufacturers are more interested in your goodwill than in saving a few dollars and will continue to allow you to return the product if you encounter a serious problem within a reasonable period, and if tech support cannot find a solution. Sometimes the support person is able to authorize or request a refund, or it may be necessary to speak with a manager. It may be that your problem appeared some time before the ultimate decision is made to return the product; in this case it should be possible to argue that as long as the first problem call occurred within the warranty period you qualify for a re-fund—another reason to keep notes!

When manufacturers just say no, refusing what you believe is a reasonable request for a refund or other satisfaction, assertiveness is often rewarded with a final victory. Escalating your complaint upwards from line personnel in customer service to their managers and higher managers may be necessary. When telephone contacts get you nowhere it's time to start a letter-writing campaign. Boris Beizer, an authority on software quality, lists 12 guidelines for effective complaints in his book *The Frozen Keyboard: Living with Bad Software* (TAB Books, 1988).

1. Don't complain about missing features—that belongs in a positive letter of suggested improvements. Unless of course, the missing features are essential and you were led to believe that they existed.

2. Document all bugs and technical problems.

3. Group your complaints into bugs, manuals, insults, clumsiness, cockpit [user] error, induction, misleading information, etc. Use screen dumps and specific examples for each case.

4. Avoid generalized bitches. Be as specific as possible. It's better to have a twenty-page letter of specific gripes than a two-page letter of generalized complaints. Put yourself in the software developer's place. He'd rather respond to substantive specifics than to generalized philosophy.

5. Do make specific suggestions for improvement or corrections. If a prompt is misleading, give them an alternate, more precise prompt to use. If the program's response is insulting, show them how to say it better.

6. Don't wave the competitor in their face. They know all about the competitive products and understand their strengths and weaknesses better than you do.

7. Be realistic. Don't expect satisfaction and compensation for consequential damages.

8. Don't expect gratitude, credit, or feedback. Consider yourself lucky if you get a form letter back that acknowledges that you sent them something. If the package is changed, you'll know if your letter had an impact. It's not that the vendors are ungrateful, but that their legal position makes it almost impossible for them to safely acknowledge your contribution.

9. Insist on a no-cost update and/or upgrade. Ask when the revised version will be available.

10. Don't whine.

11. Be sure the problem is theirs, rather than yours. All you need is to complain about one cockpit error which is your fault (unless you can clearly show how the package misled you into the error) to have the whole letter dumped into the wastebasket.

12. Don't threaten a lawsuit. If it's that serious, let your lawyer write the letter.

Beizer recommends using a cover letter addressed to the recipient along with a report containing technical material. In addition to the manufacturer of the product, possible recipients of your complaints might be the retailer you purchased from (who may have made some inflated claims) and influential third parties like the computer press. Several computer magazines have consumer affairs columns and we've all seen letters to the editor complaining of problems with manufacturers that brought results. Needless to say, you have to gauge the effort required to aggressively pursue your well-founded complaints against the possible rewards, but winning a righteous battle against an arrogant opponent can be very satisfying.

Winning the Support Game

Smart consumers keep support quality in mind when they make purchase decisions. You may have to dig to find out how the products you're considering are going to be supported, but it's worth some trouble to improve your chances of getting help when the inevitable disaster strikes, probably at the worst possible time. No matter how good the support, though, you don't want to call for help at the first sign of trouble. Try some basic troubleshooting yourself, simplifying the situation as much as possible and thinking through what you're doing carefully. When you do need to call for help, make sure you're prepared with basic information about your system and the symptoms you're concerned with. Consider support alternatives such as bulletin boards and fax lines when it's tough to get through to a human being. When you do get through to a support person, start out with a clear, concise description of what you're trying to do and what's happening instead. Try to develop some rapport with the tech person and work cooperatively to sort things out. Be assertive about what you need to get back to work productively, and be persistent if you don't feel your problem is getting sufficient attention. It may take some work, but you should be able to get quality help if you do your part.

Resources

Association of Worldwide Software Support Managers (AWWSM)
Pioneer Chapter
P.O. Box 50786
Palo Alto, CA 94303

Association for Computer Training and Support
Sagamore Road
Raquette Lake, NY 13436

The CompuMentor Project
385 8th Street, 2nd Floor
San Francisco, CA 94110

Help Desk Institute
1755 Telstar Drive, Suite 101
Colorado Springs, CO 80920

Annual Conference on Software Support
c/o Institute for International Research
427 Madison Avenue, 23rd Floor
New York, NY 10022

Software Support Professionals Association
11828 Rancho Bernardo Road, Building 123-161
San Diego, CA 92128

Bibliography

Albrecht, Karl. *Service Within: Solving the Middle Management Leadership Crisis*. Homewood, IL: Dow Jones-Irwin, 1990.

Beizer, Boris. *The Frozen Keyboard: Living with Bad Software*. Blue Ridge Summit, PA: TAB Books, 1988.

Davidow, William H., and Bro Uttal. *Total Customer Service*. New York: Harper & Row, 1989.

Evans, Tom. *The Software Support Handbook*. Los Altos, CA: Business Knowledge, 1987.

Goodman, Gary S. *Winning by Telephone: Telephone Effectiveness for Business Professionals and Consumers*. Englewood Cliffs, NJ: Prentice-Hall, 1982.

Kausen, Robert. *Customer Satisfaction Guaranteed*. Trinity Center, CA: Life Education, 1989.

Mager, Robert F. *Troubleshooting: The Troubleshooting Course*. Belmont, CA: David S. Lake Publishers, 1982.

Pines, Ayala, and Elliot Aronson. *Career Burnout: Causes and Cures*. New York: Free Press, 1988.

Rose, Bill. *Managing Software Support*. San Diego: Software Support Professionals Association, 1990.

Index

Colophon

This book was created with PageMaker 4 on a Macintosh, using Monotype's Bembo and Adobe's Franklin Gothic typeface families. The kerning pairs for Monotype Bembo were imported from Bitstream's Garamond family, and adjusted with the Pairs kerning editor.

Final output was to a LaserMAX 1000 personal typesetter, courtesy of Mike Dreis, Bill Neuenschwander, and LaserMAX Systems.

Cover design by Ted Mader + Associates.

Internal design by Olav Martin Kvern.

Production by Neil S. Kvern.

More from Peachpit Press...

The Little PC Book
Larry Magid

Here's a painless way to become PC literate without being buried in details. This book won rave reviews from *The Wall Street Journal, Business Week,* and dozens of other publications. $17.95 *(384 pages)*

The Little Online Book
Alfred Glossbrenner

A beginner's guide to everything you need to begin exploring the electronic universe from your desktop. Covers modems, the Internet, and online services. Also includes a step-by-step cookbook explaining common online tasks. $17.95 *(380 pages)*

The Little Mac Book, 3rd Edition
Robin Williams

This worldwide bestseller explains the basics of operating a Mac. You'll find new information on System 7.1, CD-ROM drives, networking, the Performa series, and more. $16.00 *(336 pages)*

The Macintosh Bible, 5th Edition
Edited by Darcy DiNucci

Now completely updated, this classic is crammed with tips, tricks, and shortcuts that cover the most current software and hardware. New chapters highlight multimedia, children's software, PowerPCs, and more. $30.00 *(1,170 pages)*

The Macintosh Bible CD-ROM
Edited by Jeremy Judson

A dazzling array of special goodies, featuring more than 600 MB of utilities, games, sounds, video clips, photos, clip art, fonts, and demos. $25.00 *(CD-ROM)*

The Macintosh Bible "What Do I Do Now?" Book, 3rd Edition
Charles Rubin

This new edition includes material on repair software and troubleshooting for all Macs. It also covers how to solve common problems in widely used Macintosh programs. $22.00 *(408 pages)*

 For a complete list of Peachpit Press titles call 1-800-283-9444 and ask for a copy of our catalog.

The Non-Designer's Design Book
Robin Williams

This book is for anyone who needs to design, but who has no background or formal training in the field. Follow these basic principles and your work will look more professional. Full of design exercises and quizzes. $14.95 *(144 pages)*

The PC Bible
Edited by Eric Knorr

The first book that dares to cover the entire universe of PCs. You'll find chapters on hardware, networking, software, telecommunications, fonts, personal finance graphics, and more. $24.95 *(900 pages)*

The PC is not a typewriter
Robin Williams

Here are the principles behind the techniques for creating professional typesetting using the PC. Topics include punctuation, leading, special characters, kerning, fonts, justification, and more. $9.95 *(96 pages)*

Protect Your Macintosh
Bruce Schneier

A hands-on guide that discusses all aspects of Macintosh security: backups, viruses, data protection, encryption, network security, and physical security. Includes reviews of useful products that can help you avert or recover from disaster. $23.95 *(350 pages)*

The Windows 3.1 Bible
Fred Davis

This book is a wall-to-wall compendium of tips, tricks, warnings, shortcuts, reviews, and resources that will inform, entertain, and empower Windows users of every ability level. $28.00 *(1,154 pages)*

The Windows Bible CD-ROM
Fred Davis

The complete guide to Windows 3.1 is now available on CD-ROM. Provides the most comprehensive online help available for Windows, plus over 500 MB of fonts, sounds, images, icons, utilities, games, shareware, freeware, and more. $34.95 *(CD-ROM)*

Zap! How Your Computer Can Hurt You and What You Can Do About It
Don Sellers

Learn about the variety of potential hazards of using your computer and how to reduce your risk. Includes chapters on backache, headache, radiation, and much more. $12.95 *(160 pages)*

Order Form

to order, call:

(800) 283-9444 or (510) 548-4393 or (510) 548-5991 (fax)

Qty	Title	Price	Total

Shipping	First Item	Each Additional		
UPS Ground	$ 4	$ 1	Subtotal	
UPS Blue	$ 8	$ 2	8.25% Tax (CA only)	
Canada	$ 6	$ 4	Shipping	
Overseas	$14	$14	**TOTAL**	

Name

Company

Address

City   State   Zip

Phone   Fax

❏ Check enclosed   ❏ Visa   ❏ MasterCard   ❏ AMEX

Company purchase order #

Credit card #   Exp. Date

What other books would you like us to publish?

Please tell us what you thought of this book:

Peachpit Press • 2414 Sixth Street • Berkeley, CA • 94710

MAC